Bridges to Heaven

Bridges to Heaven

How Well-Known Seekers Define and Deepen Their Connection With God

EDITED BY

Jonathan Robinson

STILLPOINT PUBLISHING

STILLPOINT PUBLISHING

Building a society that honors The Earth,
Humanity, and The Sacred in All Life.

For a free catalog or ordering information, write
Stillpoint Publishing, Box 640, Walpole, NH 03608, USA
or call
1-800-847-4014 TOLL FREE (Continental US, except NH)
1-603-756-9281 (Foreign and NH)

This book is manufactured in the United States of America.

Cover and text designed by Karen Savary.
Layout and typesetting by Sally Nichols.

Published by Stillpoint Publishing,
Box 640, Meetinghouse Road, Walpole, NH 03608

Library of Congress Number: 94-67620

ISBN: 0-913299-98-7

1 3 5 7 9 8 6 4 2

This book is printed on chlorine-free recycled paper
to save trees and preserve Earth's ecology.

To my teachers Justin and Joyce,
and to God — the ultimate teacher
(and playmate)

Contents

Acknowledgments

Contributing to a book about God seems to bring out the best in people. I am ever grateful to each of the many people I interviewed for sharing their wisdom and their heart with me. In all the interviews I conducted, a sense of the sacred was present. It was an honor to explore these profound questions with each contributor.

I especially want to thank my friend Carol Hawkins for helping to inspire this book, and for her ongoing support. I also want to thank the many people who helped create the book, such as my wonderful agent, Jim Heacock, and my transcriber and angelic girlfriend, Helena. All the people at Stillpoint were extremely supportive, with special thanks to Errol Sowers, Ann Weil Richards and my wonderful editor, Dorothy Seymour. Martin McDermott thought of the poetic title, and Jeff Herman, Benjamin Shield, Richard Carlson, and Ellen Downing all offered their loving support.

Because of space, not all the interviews I conducted could make it to the final version of the book. Yet I want to thank everyone who offered their wisdom so graciously, including Dennis Adams, Linda Gillies, John White, Arianna Starr, Michael Bromley, Timothy Leary, Jacob Glass, Joyce Vissell, and Sharon Gardner.

For permission to use quotes, I thank Marjorie Conte at New World Library, Denise Finnegan at Crown, Noemi Miller at Bantam, Charlene Saunders at Villard, and Van Der Leun and Associates.

Introduction

"God told me to stay home from work today." These were the words my friend said when I expressed surprise she was home to answer her phone. So I asked her, "How do you contact God?" Somehow, I assumed her answer would mimic my own way of seeking the Divine. It didn't. At first I thought she was joking with me, but it soon became apparent she wasn't kidding. So I asked her, "How do you *feel* God? What makes you feel most and least connected?" I kept asking her questions, and with each answer I was confronted with ideas and notions about a sacred reality that contrasted sharply with my own.

I saw then that I had two choices. I could dismiss my friend's notions and experience of the Divine, or I could learn from them. A quotation I read years back played through my mind: "More people have been killed in religious wars than all other wars combined." Human beings have a long history of becoming upset and defensive about the "proper" way to know God. Rather than pursue a self-righteous "my way is better than yours" attitude, I attempted to learn from my friend.

I found that her relationship with the Divine, although different from my own, was just as beautiful. If our Creator could be likened to a rainbow, my friend was seeing a palette of colors different from the one I had seen. The colors she described added new richness and possibilities to my own relationship with God. Once my curiosity was piqued, I began asking other people how they experienced the Divine. The first thing I noticed was the many ways we've separated "our" God from other people's God by giving different names to the same idea. It seemed to me that such names as Jesus, Allah, the Sacred, Jehovah, Krishna, the Divine, Spirit, the Higher Power, the Higher Self, the Source, and the Buddha Nature were all referring to a power greater than ourselves.

Throughout this book, you will find many of these terms used interchangeably. Do these many names we've created to refer to "God" really just represent the same thing? I don't know. Then again, I don't even know how a radio works. Of course, that doesn't keep me from tuning into music that nourishes and uplifts me. In the same way, we can tune into the Divine as a daily resource, even though we may not fully understand all the subtleties of who or what IT is.

In editing this book, my hope is to help myself and others deepen their experience of the Being we call "God." What could be more important than that? This book does not aim to define our Source but to define specific ways human beings can more intimately experience this essence. Unfortunately, the idea of God has, in recent years become a highly politicized and divisive issue. Various groups have attempted to force their own ideas about God on others. Yet in this age of spiritual poverty, what we really need is to learn from each other's experience. I believe that only with a humble heart and a desire to learn can we grow into a deeper relationship with the Sacred.

INNER TECHNOLOGY

When learning about any field of interest, the quickest way to learn is to study with an expert. When it comes to the Divine, the "experts" are those who demonstrate in their actions and their experience an intimate relationship with a sacred reality. By that definition, each of the people interviewed in this book is an expert. Their answers provide a "state of the art" account of the way human beings deepen their connection to God. Just as conventional technology can help us on the material plane, techniques of "inner technology" can help us get in touch with our divine essence.

The first ten chapters in this book present the answers to ten questions I asked people about God. These ten questions are listed below. The questions were selected on the basis of their practical value in helping readers have a more intimate relationship with their Creator. There is an old saying that "the devil is in the details." When it comes to deepening our connection to the Divine, I believe that "God is in the details." Most books that deal with our Source do not give the specific, precise, and practical ways in which we can more intimately know Him or Her. Yet, ultimately, that is what we all really want. By having experts answer precise questions about the way they deepen their connection to God, I aim to make this book of lasting practical value to you.

THE TEN QUESTIONS

1. How do you encounter God?

2. What does the experience of God feel like in your body, mind, and emotions?

3. How can you deepen your experience of God?

4. When you meditate and\or pray, how do you connect with the Divine presence?

5. Is there anything you do that seems to lessen your experience of God?

6. What beliefs have helped you to attain a better relationship with God?

7. What, if anything, do you think God wants from us?

8. How do you remember and/or tune into the sacred during your everyday life?

9. Have you experienced any miracles? If so, please describe one and tell how it has affected your faith in God.

10. If you had one piece of advice to give to someone who wanted a deeper relationship with God, what would you tell them?

A FINAL THOUGHT

You may find it of value to answer these questions for yourself. It's interesting to see how they compare to the answers that experts have given in this book. Since each question deals with a unique aspect of the spiritual journey, feel free to skip to the chapters that most interest you. I suggest that rather than reading quickly through the answers, you read the responses slowly and meditatively. Answers like these come from a sacred place deep within us. Attempt to feel the Spirit behind the words. I found certain answers to be extremely helpful in expanding my own relationship with God. I began to highlight the answers that affected me most. By highlighting such responses, I could conveniently reread them and gradually incorporate the beliefs and techniques they expressed. Perhaps you will find the same technique useful.

At times, I and other contributors to this book refer to God as "He" or "Him." Of course in doing so, we do not wish to imply that God is best represented by this pronoun. You may prefer to refer to God differently. In my own case, I chose to use the pronoun "Him" only because it is currently the more common way to refer to God.

I sincerely hope the words contained here help to inspire you to a deeper and more fulfilling relationship with our Creator.

Jonathan Robinson
Santa Barbara, California
Fall, 1994

Lynn Andrews	Jerry Jampolsky
Marilyn Atteberry	Gurucharan Singh Khalsa
Pat Boone	The Dalai Lama
Joan Borysenko	Kenny Loggins
LeVar Burton	Emmett Miller
Mantak Chia	Dan Millman
Deepak Chopra	Edgar Mitchell
Alan Cohen	Pam Oslie
Stan Dale	M. Scott Peck
Ram Dass	Peter Russell
Bruce Davis	Bernie Siegel
Wayne Dyer	Marsha Sinetar
Warren Farrell	Ron Smotherman
Robert Fulghum	Brother David Steindl-Rast
Willis Harman	Charles Tart
Richard Hatch	Mother Teresa
Louise L. Hay	Marianne Williamson

Path of the Prisoner — Mark DeFriest
Path of Terminal Illness — Jim Nissley
Path of the Healer— Meredith L. Young-Sowers
Path of the Philosopher — Robert Fulghum

The Contributors

As you read through the responses in this book, you'll get an intimate sense of each contributor's inner life. Yet, the people in this book have also brought their spiritual values into the material world. I encourage you to spend a little time "getting to know" the contributors and some of their "worldly" accomplishments. As you'll see, each contributor brings a unique background and perspective to the goal of spiritual awakening.

"We need to remember there's a reason for all our pain and struggle. We're here in this school house called Earth to find our path towards enlightenment."

LYNN ANDREWS has devoted her life to the study of age-old rituals and shamanism. She is the author of several accounts of her explorations into past lives and feminine spirituality, including *Medicine Woman, Jaguar Woman, Woman of Wyrrd, Flight of the Seventh Moon,* and *Star Woman.* She is also the author of *The Power Deck,* and of the workbook *Teachings Around the Sacred Wheel.*

"Love yourself; surround yourself with friends to remind you how perfect you are."

MARILYN ATTEBERRY has been designing and training self-esteem building workshops for adults and teenagers since 1975 . She is the co-creator and Director of Training for *The Sage Experience*, a self-esteem training system for adults, and co-owner of Associated Trainers, Inc., a company that designs workshops, transformational seminars, and leadership training. She has worked with more than 18,000 people and is known for her love, wisdom, and commitment to educating people to think and act in healthy and wholistic ways.

"No one knows you or loves you like God.
He's always waiting to hear from you, and
He does answer!"

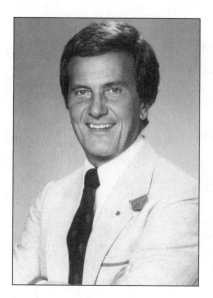

PAT BOONE a descendent of Daniel Boone, has been a singer, movie actor, author, and TV and radio show host. He is known for such hit songs as *Love Letters in the Sand* and *A Day Like Today*. He has written over a dozen books, sold more than 45 million records, starred in 15 motion pictures, starred in his own TV show, and for several years been the chairman of the Easter Seal society. His first book, *Twixt Twelve and Twenty,* sold over 800,000 copies.

"The closest we can come to the experience of the Great Mystery is to see God in one another. Remember that beyond all appearances of separation, we are one with the Heart of Love."

JOAN BORYSENKO, a medical scientist and licensed psychologist, is President of Mind/Body Health Sciences, Inc. Her vision is to integrate medicine, psychology, and spirituality. She's the author of *Minding the Body, Mending the Mind; Guilt is the Teacher, Love is the Lesson; On Wings of Light: Meditations for Awakening to the Source;* and *Fire in the Soul: A New Psychology of Spiritual Optimism.*

"After many years of training myself, strong emotions are now a trigger for me to look at something. I think that all emotions are triggers for us to grow in our level of consciousness."

LeVar Burton, although perhaps best-known for his role as Kunta Kinte in the acclaimed series, "Roots," and his current assignment as Lt. Commander Geordi La Forge in *Star Trek: The Next Generation*, initially had his sights on becoming a Catholic priest. After becoming disillusioned with religious dogma, he looked for other means to utilize his talents and humanism. He turned to acting. This has allowed him the creative room to branch out in other ways to reach the hearts and minds of his audience.

"If you want peace in the world, first have peace with yourself. Then your family, your friends, your country, and the world will have peace."

MANTAK CHIA was born in Thailand. At an early age he met Taoist Master White Cloud Hermit, and over the next five years he was taught the most sacred Taoist teachings. Master Chia has worked to create a workable energy system for Westerners that is a marriage of the best of the East and the West. He is the author of many books, including *Awaken Healing Energy Through the Tao; Taoist Secrets of Love: Cultivating Male Sexual Energy; Taoist Ways to Transform Stress Into Vitality;* and *Chi Self Massage.* He teaches courses at his Taoist healing center in Huntington, New York.

"You need to find an outlet for your love, a place where you can give it freely. The more openly you experience love, on whatever terms, the closer you will come to finding its essence."

DEEPAK CHOPRA, M.D., was born and raised in New Delhi, India. He became chief of staff at New England Memorial Hospital, and established the American Association of Ayurvedic Medicine. In 1992, Dr. Chopra was appointed to the National Institutes of Health ad hoc panel on alternative medicine. His books *Creating Health, Return of the Rishi, Quantum Healing, Perfect Health, Unconditional Life,* and *Ageless Body, Timeless Mind* have been translated into twenty-five languages.

"An intimate relationship with God takes time. The thought that I don't have time to create that space is just an illusion. As creative, masterful souls, there's always a way for us to hook up with our Source."

ALAN COHEN is a prolific and dynamic speaker and the author of many popular inspirational books, including the bestselling *The Dragon Doesn't Live Here Anymore.* Other books he has written include: *Dare to Be Yourself; The Peace That You Seek; Joy is My Compass;* and *The Healing of the Planet Earth.*

"If God wanted to hide, He would hide in human beings because that's the last place we would think to look."

STAN DALE, founder of the Human Awareness Institute, spent much of his forty-six-year career as a radio broadcaster. He was the voice of *The Shadow* and the announcer/narrator for *The Lone Ranger* and *The Green Hornet*. He has published two books, *Fantasies Can Set You Free* and *My Child, Myself—How to Raise the Child You Always Wanted to Be.* He leads workshops entitled *Sex, Love, and Intimacy,* and is a frequent guest on such shows as *Donahue* and *Oprah Winfrey.*

*"I take the assumption that every religion has been
rooted in some mystical or transcendent experience.
From that assumption, I just look at all the different
systems as metaphors or doorways to God."*

RAM DASS (a.k.a. Richard Alpert, Ph.D.) Researched the use of
psychedelics at Harvard University in the early sixties with his
colleague Timothy Leary.   In the late sixties he met his guru,
Neem Karoli Baba, in India and was renamed Ram Dass (servant
of God).   Since that time Ram Dass has done volunteer work
with various groups, including the Seva Foundation, which he
helped to form.   He has written many books, including *Be Here
Now, Grist for the Mill, Journey of Awakening, How Can I Help?* (with
Paul Gorman), and *Compassion in Action* (with Mirabai Bush).

*"Be inspired and live a life for
your soul, for eternity!"*

BRUCE DAVIS, PH.D., is the author of *Monastery Without Walls*, *The Heart of Healing*, *The Magical Child Within You*, and his favorite, *My Little Flowers*. He leads spiritual retreats around the United States and in many parts of Europe, including Assisi, Italy, and Taize, France. For information write Spring Grove, P.O. Box 807, Fairfax, California 94930.

"We are not human beings having a spiritual experience,
we are spiritual beings, having a human experience."

WAYNE DYER, PH.D. is the author of many bestsellers, including *Your Erroneous Zones, Pulling Your Own Strings, The Sky's the Limit, Gifts from Eykis, What Do You Really Want for Your Children?* and *Real Magic.* He was featured in a *Time* magazine article on "Prominent Figures in American Culture" as one to pass on his ideas to generations living a hundred years from now. Dyer has appeared on more than five thousand radio and television programs.

"Each time I eat a meal, I think of all the people whose labor has contributed to my nourishment, and that thought nourishes my appreciation. I hope it nourishes you too—three times a day."

WARREN FARRELL, PH.D., is the author of *Why Men Are the Way They Are, The Liberated Man,* and *The Myth of Male Power. Why Men Are the Way They Are,* a national bestseller, has won two national awards and is published in more than 51 countries in eight languages. The *New York Post* called it "the most important book ever written about love, sex and intimacy." His work has been featured in *Time* Magazine, the *New York Times,* and he has appeared often on shows such as *Donahue, Oprah Winfrey, Sally Jesse Raphael,* and *Geraldo.*

"Since I was told that my grandfather had died and gone to heaven, God and my grandfather got all mixed up in my mind as one and the same. Which meant I had a pretty comfy notion about God."

ROBERT FULGHUM is the author of the bestselling *All I Really Need to Know I Learned in Kindergarten, Uh-Oh,* and *It Was On Fire When I Lay Down On It.* Robert Fulghum has been a working cowboy, IBM salesman, professional artist, folksinger, minister, bartender, teacher of drawing and painting, writer and amateur philosopher. He is still working on what he wants to be when he grows up. In the meantime, he lives with his wife on a houseboat in Seattle.

"In my experience, any concept one may have of God will be a block to establishing the relationship so devoutly sought. The way to avoid such blocking is to have intention without expectation, and trust without belief."

WILLIS HARMAN is President of the Institute of Noetic Sciences in Sausalito, California. He is also Emeritus Professor of Engineering-Economic Systems at Stanford University. His personal search led him from a career in applied science to a conviction that our most important learning as individuals is to discover our true identity and purposeful life work. Dr. Harman's most recent books are *Global Mind Change: The Promise of the Last Years of the Twentieth Century*, and *Creative Work: The Constructive Role of Business in a Transforming Society*. Other books include *Changing Images of Man* and *Higher Creativity*.

"When my heart is free, unburdened, open to receiving love, I experience God. When I express this love energy in the world, I become a sacred artist translating God's energy into expression."

RICHARD HATCH has for more than two decades enjoyed international recognition as an actor. He has starred in such series as *The Streets of San Francisco* and *Battlestar Galactica*, for which he was nominated for a Golden Globe Award. He has starred in off-Broadway plays, movies for television, and feature films. Richard teaches acting and self-expression workshops throughout the country.

"See God in every person, place and thing and all will be well in your world!"

LOUISE L. HAY is the author of the international bestsellers *You Can Heal Your Life* and *The Power is Within You.* She has assisted millions of people in discovering and using the full potential of their own creative powers for personal growth and self-healing. Ms. Hay's many books and tapes have been translated into more than 25 different languages throughout the world.

"I find that when I focus each second on creating an atmosphere of unconditional love, I experience God. In my book, Love is Letting Go of Fear, *there is a cartoon caption that says 'Let's look at a person's light, not their lampshade.' "*

JERRY JAMPOLSKY, M.D. is a graduate of Stanford Medical School and a board diplomat in psychiatry. He founded the *Center For Attitudinal Healing* in Tiburon, California in 1975, and now there are more than 110 Centers and groups around the world. He has written eight books in the field of attitudinal healing and is author of the bestseller *Love Is Letting Go Of Fear.*

"The guru's job is to coordinate individuals to play their perfect note in the Divine orchestra."

GURUCHARAN SINGH KHALSA is a student and spokesperson for Yogi Bhajan, Master of Kundalini Yoga. He is a psychologist and instructor at Massachusetts Institute of Technology. He is the author of many books on Kundalini Yoga as well as a book for business called *How To Ask Effective Questions.*

"The essence of all religions is love, compassion, and tolerance. Kindness is my true religion. The clear proof of a person's love of God is if that person genuinely shows love to fellow human beings."

THE DALAI LAMA is the shortened title of His Holiness the Fourteenth Dalai Lama, Tenzin Gyatso of Tibet, one of today's most respected leaders. In 1959, nine years after China invaded Tibet, he went into exile to Dharmasala, India. He now travels throughout the world, cutting across religious, national, and political barriers, speaking of peace and humanitarian values. His life is his message. This scholar, man of peace, and spokesman for better understanding among people has written numerous books and has received many honorary degrees and awards. In 1989 the world acknowledged His Holiness by awarding him the Nobel Peace Prize.

"The Spirit speaks directly to our hearts through music. That's why music has always had such power to move people into positive action."

KENNY LOGGINS is a Grammy Award winning singer/songwriter who has sold more than 20 million records. With his former partner Jim Messina, he created eight albums, followed by six solo albums. Kenny has also contributed songs on five movie soundtracks. He is active in various charities, such as Toys for Tots and U.S.A. for Africa. He has won many humanitarian awards for his participation in projects to relieve human suffering. Most recently he has hosted a television special entitled *This Island Earth*.

"Having dealt with a lot of people, I've now demon-
strated to my satisfaction that the Divine can be
found within any person. Sometimes I find it in my
first visit with them, and sometimes it takes a year
before I can say, 'Ah, there it is...' "

EMMETT MILLER, M.D. is a pioneer in the field of integra-
tive medicine. His work is geared toward bringing a deeper
understanding of the way the mind and body can work in harmony to produce healing, balance, and wellness. He is the
author of two books, *Opening your Inner "I"* and *Self Imagery:
Creating Your Own Good Health.* Dr. Miller has produced a series
of audio and video tape programs that focus on self-healing,
personal growth, and wellness enhancement.

"Now and then I like to lift my eyes up from the details of daily life and remember the bigger picture, and take a breath of God, and feel and remember that ultimately, it's all okay."

DAN MILLMAN is a past world champion gymnast, university coach and college professor. He is the author of *Way of the Peaceful Warrior, Sacred Journey of the Peaceful Warrior, No Ordinary Moments, The Warrior Athlete* and, most recently, *The Inner Athlete.* His disillusion with "the usual life" sent him around the world and into the depths of his mind and heart. Dan is currently conducting workshops, and enjoying life with his family.

"I believe that our deepest beliefs change not only the way we relate to the world, but virtually change the physical world we live in."

EDGAR MITCHELL, PH.D. is a former astronaut, the sixth man to walk on the moon, and founder of the Institute of Noetic Sciences. He is considered a pioneer in modern efforts to expand the role of science toward understanding the inner experience. He is also the founder of the Association of Space Explorers, an educational organization developed to provide new understanding of the human condition resulting from the epoch of space exploration. He has received the Presidential Medal of Freedom and the NASA Distinguished Service Medal.

"Out of being totally willing to die, God gave me the strength to choose life."

JIM NISSLEY was in charge of training for the Southland Corporation in Central California from 1979 to 1985. In 1991, he founded "Stop AIDS Now," a nonprofit agency, and led a campaign to require warning labels on all lambskin condoms. Three pieces of AIDS related legislation he wrote have been passed by both houses of the state of California. He has been honored by the county of San Fransisco, Santa Barbara, and State Assembly and Senate. His efforts as an AIDS activist have been featured on NBC, ABC, CBS, FOX, and CNN news.

"God is as close to us as our own breath and as much a part of us as our own hearts. I believe we are aspects of God, alive to experience and express pure Love and Creativity."

PAM OLSIE is a professional psychic sensitive to the human aura. She has written a book on the aura colors entitled *Life Colors*. She travels around the country presenting workshops and appearing on numerous television and radio programs. She has also presented her information on the aura to the International Forum on New Science.

"One of the things I am continually doing during my prayer time is checking out my life with my Ideal Observer. 'Tell me, God,' I am asking, 'what I just did or what I am thinking of doing—how does it look through your eyes? Does it look civil?' "

M. SCOTT PECK, M.D. is the author of *The Road Less Traveled*, the extraordinary work that has remained on the *New York Times* bestseller list for more than eight years. His other bestsellers include *People of the Lie, The Different Drum, A World Waiting to be Born*, and the novel *A Bed by the Window*. He has also written a fable, *The Friendly Snowflake*, and is the co-author of *What Return Can I Make? Dimensions of the Christian Experience*. He lives with his wife, Lily, in Connecticut.

"We can go through our whole lives worrying about our future happiness, and totally miss where true peace lives—right here, right now."

PETER RUSSELL is a physicist from England, and the author of the bestselling book *The Global Brain.* He is also the author of *The Brain Book,* and *The White Whole in Time: Our Future Evolution and the Meaning of Now.* His video version of *The Global Brain* won several awards and became an international bestselling video. He conducts workshops across the world on spirituality and the future evolution of mankind.

"The essence of my interview can be presented by holding up a newborn child and asking, 'Any questions about our bridges to heaven?' The enlightened have no questions."

BERNIE SIEGEL, M.D. published his first book, *Love, Medicine and Miracles* in 1986. He is now involved in humanizing medical education and making the medical profession aware of the mind-body connection. In 1989 he wrote *Peace, Love, and Healing,* and in 1993, *How to Live Between Office Visits.* He is a pediatric and general surgeon, writer, teacher, and father of five children. He predicts that in a decade, the effects of consciousness on man and matter will be an accepted scientific fact.

"Just turn toward God. That's all. Adjust your attention upward. Steer your heart's movement towards That which is Divine. That is enough."

MARSHA SINETAR is one of the foremost exponents of the practical value of wholesome spirituality. She is a prolific author, and her books are increasingly used worldwide in a variety of settings. Her books include the bestsellers *Ordinary People as Monks and Mystics, Do What You Love and the Money Will Follow,* and *Developing a 21st Century Mind.* Her latest book is called *Reel Power,* and it deals with the spiritual dimension of popular movies.

"I consider life to be a training assignment. The task of this training is to live fully by striving to master the ability to be loved and the ability to be loving."

RON SMOTHERMAN is a physician who has given up his profession to answer more directly the day-by-day needs of people for the kind of material he offers. He has written *Winning Through Enlightenment, Transforming #1, The Man Woman Book, Play Ball, The Miracle of Children, Conversations With Life,* and *Handbook For the Third Millennium.* Ron conducts *The Man-Woman Training,* which has several thousand graduates in the United States, England, Russia, Germany, Switzerland, Austria, Canada, and Australia.

"I meet the Divine in humans that are very transparent towards the Divine. That can be a very profound and wonderful way of communicating with God—like darshan."

BROTHER DAVID STEINDL-RAST has, since 1953, been a monk of Mount Savior Monastery in New York. After twelve years of formal training in philosophy and theology, he received permission to practice Zen with Buddhist masters. Brother David has contributed to many books and periodicals, including the *Encyclopedia Americana* and *New Age Journal*. His current books are *Gratefulness, The Heart of Prayer* and *A Listening Heart*.

*"Whatever the truth ultimately is, I know
it's got to be more than just this constant sea of
fantasies that I generate."*

CHARLES TART, a Professor of Psychology at the University of California at Davis, is internationally famous for research with altered states, transpersonal psychology, and parapsychology. His ten books include two classics, *Altered States of Consciousness* and *Transpersonal Psychologies*. *Waking Up: Overcoming the Obstacles to Human Potential* synthesized Buddhist, Sufi, and Gurdjieffian mindfulness training ideas with modern psychology. His latest book, *Open Mind, Discriminating Mind*, extends these explorations.

"It's not how much we give, but how much love we put in the doing—that's compassion in action."

MOTHER TERESA was born in 1910 in Yugoslavia as Agnes Boyaxhui. In 1928 she joined the Loretta nuns in Ireland and soon was sent to India to do her novitiate. She founded a school in the slums, learned some basic medicine, and began treating the sick in their homes. Mother Teresa founded the Missionaries of Charity, a worldwide mission whose members follow her path, ministering to the "poorest of the poor." Her work has earned her the love and admiration of people all over the world. In 1979, she was awarded the Nobel Peace Prize.

*"Most people don't really need advice. They just
need support and discipline in doing what they
already know works."*

MARIANNE WILLIAMSON lectures internationally in the fields of
spirituality and new thought. Her teachings are based on the ideas
in *A Course in Miracles*, a self-study system of spiritual psychothera-
py. Ms. Williamson is the author of *A Return to Love* and *A Woman's
Worth*. She is the Founder and Chairman of the Board of Directors
of the Los Angeles and Manhattan Centers for Living, non-profit
organizations that provide free non-medical support services to
people living with life-challenging illnesses and grief.

"When we are unable to love and appreciate our-selves and our efforts, we run away from our mis-takes and failures, rather than learning from them."

MEREDITH L. YOUNG-SOWERS is a teacher, healer, and author of numerous books and audio tape programs in the New Consciousness/Spiritual Growth field.   Her books include: *Agartha: A Journey to the Stars, Language of the Soul, Spiritual Crisis,* and the *Angelic Messenger Cards.*   Meredith is a founder of Stillpoint Publishing and serves currently as Director of the Stillpoint Institute for Life Healing and Spiritual Community.

1

How I Encounter God

*"I am satisfied that when the Almighty
wants me to do or not do any particular
thing, He finds a way of letting me know it."*
ABRAHAM LINCOLN

If you watch shows like *Donahue* and *Geraldo*, you've witnessed frank discussion on some pretty delicate subjects. Guests openly discuss such things as being addicted to child pornography, having sex with animals, and other outrageous topics. Yet even on shows like these, talking about God is considered too controversial! The fact of the matter is, people have very strong beliefs about God, and they don't like to hear other beliefs that may challenge their own view.

A belief system is an interesting phenomena. A *belief* is a feeling of certainty about something. When we say we have

a belief in God or that we believe a friend is honest, we're saying we feel pretty certain about such things. Yet, we often
develop strong beliefs about things we have no direct experience with. In seminars I lead for example, I frequently take out
a two-foot-long needle and an ordinary balloon. I ask the audience, "How many people here believe you can put a needle all
the way through a balloon without its popping?" Usually no
hands are raised. I then ask, "How many people here have tried?"
Once again, no hands raised. I then proceed to do the "impossible." In fact, you can too. All you need do is put the needle
through the two ends of the balloon, where the rubber is just a
little bit thicker. What's interesting is the way we commonly create ironclad beliefs that are based on no direct experience at all.

No matter how people experience God, there is a tendency
for them to believe that the *way* they find God is the *best* way.
If they encounter God while hopping on one foot in the rain on
a Thursday, they will likely think such a practice is *the* way to
know God ("Hey, you should *try* it, it's the *only* way). I call this
tendency "belief blindness." Throughout history, prolonged
wars have been caused by people demanding that others
encounter God in the same way they do. Nowadays, "belief
blindness" rarely results in wars, but it can lead to something just
as damaging: it prevents people from exploring new and poten-
tially beneficial ways of experiencing their Creator.

While it's easy to disagree with people concerning their
beliefs about God, it's much harder to invalidate their *experience*.
By asking people about the way(s) they experience or
encounter God, I hoped to avoid the trap of discussing differing religious *beliefs*. As you will see by the answers I received,
people encounter God in an amazing variety of ways. Some
people encounter the Higher Power through time in nature, or
time alone in meditation and prayer. Other people experience
God through their contact with spiritual beings of various
types, or with people they love. And still others have rather
unique ways of encountering their Creator.

Think of the responses that follow as a "menu" for the many ways people relate to and encounter God. Some of them you will surely be familiar with, while others will seem rather odd. By exploring many different paths to God, it's possible for us to encounter our Creator more frequently and deeply than ever before.

❀ ❀

How Do You Encounter God?

LYNN ANDREWS

I encounter God through nature. If I am in a place of agitation or I need to move back to my center, I just go outside and feel the wind in my face. The wind is an ally for me. When it comes to me, I begin to feel deep serenity. I also encounter the Great Spirit through beauty. Watching the light on the leaves of a tree, or reflected off bamboo is a way I move into the sacred dream time.

I experience God through the help of my allies. In the study of shamanism as I have learned it from the Sisterhood of the Shields, "allies" are energy forms that give us strength and help. They also encourage and protect us. Different religions and cultures have given these energies different names, from leprechauns and angels to guwawas or little green men. Performing ceremonies in which I ask these energies to come in is another way I encounter the Great Spirit.

MARILYN ATTEBERRY

Yesterday I became a grandmother for the third time. Eye contact with my laboring daughter, holding her hand, breathing with her, is looking into the face of God. Holding my granddaughter, her fingers around my pinkie, her 16-hour-old eyes looking into mine, her mouth making tiny sucking sounds, is feeling the heart of the Divine. Listening to my two-and-a-half-year-old grand-daughter telling my 82-year-old dad about the joys of being a "big sister" is hearing the voice of God speak to God.

I'm lucky in my work because I am continually in the pres-ence of people as they let down the armor around their hearts and allow themselves to love themselves as innocent, worthy, capable children of God. Each time that occurs, I stand in the presence of God. Every time I think of that happening, I experience the Divine. Writing about it, I experience God.

And, of course, being with the awesome beauty of nature (Mount Shasta, the ocean, a rose,) takes me to the house of God ... marveling over modern technology takes me to the mind of God ... falling asleep "spooned" around my husband takes me to the very soul of God.

PAT BOONE

Quite simply, I raise my hands upward, visualizing my Heavenly Father and take a long, slow, deep breath. It feels wonderful, physically, but I'm literally asking the Lord to fill my lungs with His breath. I believe He does! As I exhale, I breathe His name, express thanks in simple ways, and often speak words of praise and endearment. I breathe this way a number of times, receiving His spirit/breath, and use the exhalation to voice my feelings toward Him. Sometimes I'll even ask for His forgiveness in certain specific areas, and it feels good to get the "dirty stuff" out of my system, along with the stale air. I don't have adequate words to tell you how much good this exercise does for me.

Now—most mornings, after my physical and spiritual exercises, I try to sit down and let Him speak directly to me out of His Word, the Bible. Just reading one of those Psalms out loud brings me into honest, authentic praise, and that's not always easy for me as an average human being. I let the Psalmist David "prime my pump," and from there I usually move into specific prayer, asking God to help me and others who have particular needs.

JOAN BORYSENKO

I experience God in nature and behind the eyes of every person I meet when I'm fully aware. When I'm stuck in my own fears, what I see in other people are my judgments. But when my heart is open, what I see in other people is the Divine. Because I have fewer judgments about them, I find it particularly easy to see God in babies. In India they take the darshan (spiritual blessings) of saints. I think we can have the darshans of babies and have a similar experience.

I recognize the divine presence in any moment when I'm fully and completely present to life. When I see the beauty of a sunset, or I completely listen to another person, I experience holy moments. Sometimes I do it with pets. Pets have a way of bringing me totally into the present moment. By simply having a firmly rooted desire and intention to experience the divine presence, you will find that it can happen, both in daily life and in periods of quiet and meditation.

LEVAR BURTON

I experience God with a thought, a breath, or an activity of puja (ritualistic worship). Anything can be a trigger that causes me to remember God—and that I am God. One thing I do is to create altars wherever I am. They trigger my stopping and acknowledging the presence of God in my life. I have an altar in my house, in my office, in my car, and in my trailer at work. I have a traveling altar space for being on the road. On the altars, I place objects that hold power and meaning for me. Sometimes I take objects from them and use them in ceremony. I love ceremonies. Creating and maintaining these altars helps me encounter God.

MANTAK CHIA

It could be said that the way I encounter God is by having sex with God. Let me explain: in human beings, men have what is called "yang chi" (male energy) and women have "yin chi" (female energy). In sex, these energies are reunited. But in the Taoist way, you learn to develop both the male and female energy inside yourself. We call this "self-intercourse," and all the great master monks and nuns do this. When you can do this self-intercourse, you give birth to yourself. That's what Jesus meant when he said, "You must be born again." When these two energies reunite and become one inside yourself, you give birth to your immortal spirit. I encounter God by reuniting my own immortal spirit with the Holy Spirit. It could be said that I marry or have sex with God, and in so doing get to experience heaven.

DEEPAK CHOPRA

You can learn to take your awareness into the region of timelessness at will—meditation is the classic technique for mastering this experience. In meditation the active mind is withdrawn to its source; just as this changing universe had to have a source beyond change, your mind, with all its restless activity, arises from a state of awareness beyond thought, sensation, emotion, desire, and memory. This is a profound personal experience.

ALAN COHEN

I experience God in meditation when I release the thoughts that are unlike God. While meditating, I realize that God has always been there, but that I needed to let go of what wasn't God. I find God in relationships. I find God in nature. I find God in moments of creativity when I'm writing or when I'm teaching. Those are the primary routes that God uses now to come to me.

STAN DALE

How can you not encounter God? How can you not breathe? God is the breath that's in us, it's the energy and the blood that flows through us. Everything that we are is about God. Every time I see a human being, I see myself, and I see God. I do a silent "Namaste," which is a greeting given in India. The greeting means "The God in me acknowledges the God in you." My entire life is committed to doing God's work—which is healing the planet and being in love 24 hours a day.

RAM DASS

I encounter God as a seductive sense of something just behind the veils of form. Hanuman, who is part of the Hindu pantheon, says, "When I don't know who I am, I serve God. When I do know who I am, I am God." That describes the funny in-and-out quality of my experience of God. When I'm feeling separate, I see God in everything around me. I look at people, and I see them as God in disguise. But when I am quiet in meditation and I experience gratitude for the grace of it all, I allow my unworthiness to go, so that I can start to feel as if God and I are one.

BRUCE DAVIS

I lead spiritual retreats, and during that time we focus on feeling our inner peace and let go of the physical and emotional stuff we have going on in our lives. Sometimes I lead retreats to certain special places or people. I've met many special people—from India, the Philippines, and Europe, but (the Master) Sai Baba is in a separate category. What's interesting to me is how deeply he touches people, and how much he inspires people to service. He teaches about the importance of service, devotion, and character. Those are the main ways he teaches people to encounter God.

Nowadays, I find the service I do helps me to encounter God. I think service is important because we're always working on ourselves, but service helps take the "edge" off. It helps us realize that everything we give to others we also give to ourselves. It takes away the veneer that makes us feel that we're somehow separate from the rest of the world. And service really breaks through selfishness; it breaks through the crust around our hearts.

WAYNE DYER

I've experienced God most often in my life during times of crises. In those times, I've gotten very quiet and peaceful. There was a time, about a decade ago, when I was going through a tough time in my marriage. We were even talking about splitting up. I can remember in my own sadness, getting very quiet and peaceful. In my speeches and TV appearances, I was much more compassionate and caring. I realized that during this time I was saying, "God, talk to me." Looking back, I can see that what we label as "crises" are really just great learning opportunities.

WARREN FARRELL

When I go out at night and look at all the stars in the sky, I feel the power of the billions of stars and the enormous humility that comes from being—I imagine— just one little speck of energy in a gigantic infinity. I feel awed by the mystery of being both so finite and yet so infinite, so much and so little, so conscious and yet, so coincidental. For me, the massiveness of what I don't know creates one way I experience God. It creates in me a feeling of humility and a sense of gratitude for being given the gift of life.

WILLIS HARMAN

I experience the deeper reality, the all-pervading spirit, intensely in rare and unbidden brief periods of extreme clarity of perception. This is encountering God.

RICHARD HATCH

I experience God whenever I express my truth in the world— and that is when I have the courage to stand up and express the energy that's inside my heart. I might sing it, dance it, write it, or simply look in someone's eyes and share it. When I communicate from my heart what I feel and know to be true with another, I feel free, uninhibited, limitless. When I hold back any part of myself, I feel just the opposite.

Every performer lives to experience that moment of total surrender, the moment when he or she lets go and feels the power and glory of God. Others may not call it God, but the experience is just the same. You feel this tremendous peace, love, and power welling up inside you. It takes courage to step up in front of the crowd and express yourself. But when your heart is beating and the adrenaline is flowing, you have enough energy to move out of the straight-jacket we live in and touch the magic. It is then that I experience the majesty of God's Being in me.

LOUISE HAY

I see God, the Life Essence, expressed in every flower, every rock, and every person, place and thing on this planet. I often say to a tree, "Good morning, God. How beautiful you are today." I bless my food with love and thank it for giving its life force to nourish me. When I ask for something and receive it, I am aware that I have cooperated with the Laws of Life and that God, the Lawmaker of Life, has responded to me. It is then that I say "Thank you" with great gratitude to the Universe.

JERRY JAMPOLSKY

I find that when I focus each second on creating an atmosphere of unconditional love, I experience God. I try not to judge people, and instead I listen to them and focus on their inner light. In my book, *Love is Letting Go of Fear,* there is a cartoon caption that says, "Let's look at a person's light, not their lampshade." I think many people look at a person's costume, and then judge whether that person is guilty or innocent, good or bad, worthy or unworthy of love.

I have encountered God in many ways, including in nature and during gardening. A couple of years ago I got an inner message to stay in Australia for a whole month without communicating with the outside world. My ego said, "How stupid can you be! There's too much to do." But as I spent time in nature, I began to talk to the trees and really slow down. I would work all day in the garden and really experience a whole different way of being. I had written books about connecting with the Source, but in Australia I began to experience it in a much deeper way. So now, when I fly places to lecture, I always take time to go for a walk in nature. It's a way of nourishing my soul. I find the laws of God and the laws of love right there in nature.

The Dalai Lama

There are two ways to enter into Buddhism: one through faith and one through reasoning. Faith alone may not be sufficient. Buddha always emphasized a balance of wisdom and compassion: a good brain and a good heart should work together. Placing importance on just the intellect and ignoring the heart can create more problems and more suffering in the world. On the other hand, if we emphasize the heart and ignore the brain, then there is not much difference between humans and animals. These two must be developed in balance, and when they are, the result is material progress accompanied by good spiritual development. Heart and mind working in harmony will yield a truly peaceful and friendly human family.

Kenny Loggins

God speaks through me through love. God sings to me, through me. God holds me in Her arms at night, and my heart opens again and again. I receive the gift of the love in Her eyes. God is the grace of insight; God is the courage to let go.

Emmett Miller

I encounter God in working with people, especially patients and students who are engaged in honest struggle with major life challenges. In the heat of their battle, I become aware of the divine presence. I remember the words of some chap who said, "Whenever two or more are gathered in My name. . . . " Yet the name does not have to be Yahweh or Jesus but simply the name of that which is nameless.

I also discover that presence when I'm alone in the desert, hundreds of miles away from any machines or noise. I feel that presence when treking in Nepal, when making love with my wife, or when I'm involved with my children in a deep and caring way. Seeing the honesty and purity my children bring into the world helps me to be in touch with the divine presence.

DAN MILLMAN

It seems to me that beliefs create experience and that God takes on the shapes of our conceptual containers. In my case, because my belief/experience envisions the Universe as the container, I experience God everywhere—within and without—but my experience itself varies between complete forgetfulness to intimate contact, depending upon how open my heart and feelings and attention are in any moment.

PAM OSLIE

How I experience God has been a dilemma for me lately. Because of old training, I used to think of God as separate from me, and I believed that I needed to be careful and a good girl so that God would love me. Now my view is shifting into experiencing God as a part of me, a presence that's right here inside of me, outside of me, everywhere. So now I experience God as a loving presence or force that is everywhere.

I encounter God in my prayers. I'm amazed at how quickly my prayers get answered now. I'll ask for help, and Bam! If I was feeling depressed before, all of a sudden the emotions will lift. I just ask for help and honestly release it to God, and my emotional state changes so quickly. And nothing logical has happened. Somebody didn't come to rescue me, money didn't fall from the sky. Nothing physically has happened, but the negative energy just leaves and I find myself in a higher space—more peaceful and happy.

BERNIE SIEGEL

God and I are so close that God is a part of my life. We're always talking to each other. I look at nature, I look at trees turning color in the Fall, and I say, "Why bother to turn color? Why not just fall on the ground?" I look at ice floating and I say, "Why do you do that?" No other liquid when frozen becomes less dense and floats; others all become heavier. And when I answer these questions, I become closer to and experience God. What do I mean? I mean that what is happening says to me that leaves turn color so that we will get the message that before we let go of the tree of life, we need to show our beauty. Ice floats because our planet would not survive if everything froze from the bottom up. These things show me that we are loved. In God I trust.

MARSHA SINETAR

I encounter God as a living Triune Person and as an infinite Holy Spirit that loves me. I encounter God *gratefully* — as a loving, searing, eternal Heart, stirring mine to life in a sanctifying, mysterious, and wholly supernatural way.

BROTHER DAVID STEINDL-RAST

I experience God in all situations that evoke awe in me. This frequently occurs in nature, particularly in the mountains or the desert. It also occurs in the arts, particularly music, poetry, theater, and painting. These art forms frequently inspire me to feel great awe. In such moments, I feel a communion with the Ultimate.

I meet the Divine in humans who are very transparent towards the Divine. That can be a profound and wonderful way of communicating with God—like darshan (the blessing of a holy person). Being with pets can often be a very prayerful activity as well. Animals are the highest form of aliveness that are still spontaneously transparent to the Divine. Humans have to work at that. Meeting an animal can be quite similar to meeting a very saintly person. They are totally transparent. When I look at a cat, it's like looking into God's eyes.

CHARLES TART

I'm very uncomfortable with the term "God." I've been trying to explore my discomfort with that. It's not that I have difficulty with other people talking about God, and it's not that I don't believe in God. It's that while I can tap into a mode of experience that I think is deeper or higher or more important than my ordinary mode, it doesn't fit the conventional category of God very well. Experiencing God is not like having some intelligent being speaking to me. So when I say I experience—let's say the "Greater," I mean I come to my senses in a very literal way. Either deliberately through some practices or simply spontaneously as a gift, I let go of the constant drivenness of my thoughts, and things relax and open up.

*"Silence is the language God speaks, and
everything else is a bad translation."*
FATHER THOMAS KEATING

2
What God Feels Like

"The knowledge of God is very far from the love of Him."
PASCAL

Does the "experience of God" feel the same for a Moslem and a Christian? Does the experience of God always feel the same for a given individual? How does one know they are in contact with God in the first place? These were some of the questions I hoped to have answered when asking people about what God felt like in their bodies, minds, and emotions.

When it comes to our relationship with God, the tendency is to focus on the ways that we're different from other people. Yet do we actually experience God differently? Perhaps people *feel* God in very similar ways but just have different methods and beliefs that help them to contact their Source. After reading the answers experts gave to this question, you can decide for yourself.

The people I interviewed for this book are committed spiritual seekers. They therefore attribute certain intense feelings they have to being in contact with God. To satisfy my own curiosity, I also asked people who considered themselves agnostics and atheists if they ever felt similar feelings. In general, their answer was "no." While many said they sometimes felt deep feelings of peace or love, they reportedly lacked the experience of feeling connected to something much larger than themselves. Many "nonbelievers" were even surprised to find that other people really DO experience the intensity and range of feelings that are described in this chapter. In addition, I found that nonbelievers interpreted their feelings of peace, joy, and love in a different manner than do people who believe in God. They would report, for instance, that their feelings of peace are due to a "nondivine" source, such as the tranquillity of being in nature.

If you've ever read a romantic novel, you know how an erotic description of a couple making love can be quite stimulating; memories of our own sexual encounters can be stirred up, leading to a feeling of sensuous arousal. In a similar way, reading about how other people describe their experience of God can trigger our own memories of divine intimacy. As you read the varied descriptions that follow, allow yourself to reminisce about times you've experienced similar feelings and sensations.

What does the experience of God feel like in your body, mind, and emotions?

LYNN ANDREWS

The experience of God feels like flying. It feels as if I'm walking above the ground with such equilibrium that nothing can sway me from my path. In my mind, I watch what I and others do. I look out through the eyes of the sacred witness. It's like being the eye of the storm. I see without judgment or opinion. I just watch as everything passes in and out of my awareness like clouds.

MARILYN ATTEBERRY

The "experience of God" brings a sense of peace and a feeling that "all's well in the world," to my body, mind and emotions. I remember tough times—sons battling cancer; the possible break-up of my marriage; feeling betrayed and misunderstood—and beyond the fear was the consistent sound of a surf-like feeling that said, "Be still and know I am God" that allowed me to sleep and trust and forgive and keep on loving. There's a feeling of grace that undulates through my body with tingles and rushes when love and self-forgiveness becomes palpable in the seminar room. Often, laughter is irresistible.

JOAN BORYSENKO

Experiencing God gives me a sense of tremendous peacefulness and love—of losing my boundaries. I feel connected with something much larger than myself. I feel very much alive, as if I can feel the life force in every cell of my body. I believe that such experiences are really the healing state in which the body can regain homeostasis. By coming into the present moment, we allow the body to come back to that state in which the innate intelligence of every cell can express itself. But perhaps the most delicious experience of God is feeling completely held, supported, and infused with a love beyond words: like the feeling that the psalmist wrote of: being held in the palm of God or being wrapped in the wings of angels. Safe and content.

LeVar Burton

In my mind, God feels like a voice that is strong and clear. It comes through especially when I put myself in a quiet place and ask an important question. As doubt comes up in my mind, the Voice repeats itself. It is definitely different from my normal mind chatter. It feels singular. My mind chatter tends to take on the resonance of a chorus. But the voice of God is singular in its expression. In my body, I feel as if all my chakras are aligned. It feels as if I'm being breathed by a greater power.

Deepak Chopra

In the state of timelessness or transcendent awareness, you have the sensation of fullness. In place of change, loss, and decay, there is steadiness and fulfillment. You sense that the infinite is everywhere; the fears associated with change disappear; the fragmentation of eternity into seconds, hours, days, and years becomes secondary, and the perfection of every moment becomes primary.

Alan Cohen

Experiencing the Divine brings a feeling of peace. Sometimes it's a very quiet peace and sometimes it's a joyful exhilaration. When I'm meditating, my body gets very quiet, my mind becomes porous. It's like opening up the windows of a room on a spring day. The old winter stuffiness gets blown away by the fresh breeze. And when I'm teaching, I get really excited, and ideas will start to come through me. Sometimes I have so much energy I won't know exactly what to do with it. My heart opens, and I feel light and lively and humorous. All the switches are turned on.

Stan Dale

Feeling God is like breathing. How do I know I'm breathing unless I stop and think, "Oh, I'm breathing." When I experience the Divine I have such energy—I'm filled with God's love. My life is just one phenomenal energy. I have about five hours of sleep each night, to the chagrin of the people I work with. When I wake up, I feel like saying "Good morning, everybody! I'm alive, I'm awake, I'm alert and enthusiastic!" I've got this ball of energy because I'm filled with the Holy Spirit. It motivates my day, my actions, my being. It feels so natural.

RAM DASS

When I enter into that quality of Oneness, there's a very big shift in the whole feeling inside my body. It's as if I come back into my body and feel it as very vitally alive. The energy is finer energy. I feel myself tuning into the balances of the way I sit or stand in order to let go of any energy blockages. My mind becomes empty of fascination or clinging to any form. Like waves, thoughts rise up and then dissolve back into the ocean. Yet, the experience is that of being the ocean instead of the waves.

As to my emotions, those we call happy or sad dissolve into a quality of emotional fullness in which it feels as if every emotion is present all at once. In other words, if somebody were to say, "Are you sad?" I'd say "Yeah." And if that person said, "Are you happy?" I'd say "Yeah." Both emotions are there. In being with the universe, there's a knowing that there is both incredible suffering and incredible joy happening in the world—and you're part of it all. To deny any of it is to deny yourself, because there is only God.

WAYNE DYER

What does God feel like? It's like being high. It's a giddy, euphoric feeling without the toxic side effects of taking drugs. It's a feeling of lightness, like having a warm shower running inside me. I almost feel as if I can defy gravity. When I lift my feet, it's as though they're weightless. It's like moon walking.

It's a very consuming pleasure and a sense that everything is okay. It can happen even in moments of pain or discomfort.

WARREN FARRELL

Experiencing God feels like a combination of being irrelevant, small, inconspicuous, and humble, and being everything, all-important, powerful, and grateful. It's an inner peace that comes from looking at life as an experience to be enjoyed—almost like a creative game, always playing hard as if winning counted, while always knowing that winning doesn't count and that even the choice to play is mine.

RICHARD HATCH

In those moments when I am fully open to receiving and expressing, every particle of my being, every cell, every organ is aligned and vibrating with God's energy. I'm glowing. I'm like a light bulb. I'm like an actor on stage who can do no wrong. I'm like a surfer in the pocket of a wave. It's a moment of total surrender, joy, and fulfillment.

WILLIS HARMAN

Experiencing God gives me the most profound feeling of love, beauty, and awe; awareness of being one with the Creator and Creation; total trust and inner peace.

JERRY JAMPOLSKY

The experience of God is beyond words. Yet, if I had to describe it, I'd say it's an effervescence of spirit, a zest for life, a sense of inspiration that comes from the universe. When I experience God I feel as if angels are hovering over me. Along with all that, there is a sense of awe for the miracles that continue to occur all around.

GURUCHARAN SINGH KHALSA

What does God feel like? It's like a kiss without end. It's like seeing the ocean for the first time. It's like when you first love someone and you look in that person's eyes and you find the Infinite in the present moment. At such moments, my body goes through changes—tingling, opening, lightness; feeling connected to everything. There's a sense of clarity about what I should do. There's a sense of completeness, grace, and seamless action.

KENNY LOGGINS

God feels calm, truly trusting that what I need I get—and I get nothing I'm not ready for. Understand that the experience of Spirit is not linear and, as such, is full of contradiction. Magic wouldn't be Magic if it were linear. Love is beyond the mind, but words are the mind's creation. The mind would have us believe that everything must be contained within words. But Love is the Paradox, and God is but Love.

DAN MILLMAN

When I open to the Mystery that is the experience of God, I feel a rising sense of joy and peace in my chest. My body relaxes and feels light and transparent. Everything feels absolutely ókay, like as if this were the most important thing.

EMMETT MILLER

Experiencing God feels like I am an ocean of tears. I can feel all the sadness of every sentient being that's ever been. It feels as if I can sense the joyful quality of the life force as it expresses itself in a child going down a water slide. It's a triumphant scream of wholeness and total abandon to the feeling of joy. I feel a sense of enormous power, as though I am standing shoulder to shoulder and marching forward with every other human being alive. And, finally, I feel completely insignificant. All those feelings happen at the same time.

PAM OSLIE

Depending on whether I'm perceiving God as separate from me or within me, experiencing God feels different. I even get different sensations. When I perceive God as being separate from me, I feel humility. It can bring me to tears. When I think of God as within me, I experience it as total acceptance and love. There's an emotion of power, of magnificence, and my body doesn't even feel as though it exists. Of course, my mind gets very quiet. If my mind's not quiet, I don't experience God as much as I think about God.

PETER RUSSELL

Rather than talk about what God feels like to me, I tend to talk about what my innermost essence feels like. When I experience my essence, or my preferred state of consciousness, I feel at peace in myself. The psycho-social fears that inhibit my mind much of the time are no longer there. I'm not talking about biological fears. If you're about to be run over by a bus, you need to feel fear. I'm talking about the "what will other people think of me?" type of fears. When I'm in my essence, my mind doesn't worry. I'm in the present moment. I'm open to observing what is going on around me. Normally, my attention is on what I did yesterday or what might happen in the future.

When I experience my essence, I'm more loving toward other people and myself. My mind doesn't make judgments. I accept life as I was meant to experience it—before I got caught up in all the concerns that society gets us involved in. It's a state in which I know exactly what is appropriate to do and communicate. In that sense, it's a much more spontaneous state of consciousness than I experience normally.

BERNIE SIEGEL

Well, the first word that comes to me about the experience of God is peace. I feel loved, I feel cared for, and peace comes with that— no matter how difficult the situation.   The experience of God is like always having sunshine in the midst of the greatest adversity.

I also have the experience of what I call a spiritual flat tire.   If I'm going to the airport and I have a plane to catch, and I get a flat tire, I get angry and upset if I miss the plane. But while waiting for a later flight, I learn that the plane I missed crashed. So I go out and I embrace my tire and I bronze it and I hang it over my fireplace. Experiences like this help me understand that some of the things I experience are God, even though I may not like what happens.

MARSHA SINETAR

In the "natural" (as the evangelists put it) my experience of God is "empty." It's still. Rich. Thought-less. Commotion-less. Intelligent. I identify strongly with Martin Buber's sentiment that this transcendent experience is both "sumptuous and stingy; heaps up abundance and refuses encompassment." I feel indescribable wonder and then no-thing. Now no-thing, now form; now formless, now form; now incomprehensible stillness and peace, now no-thing. This repeating cycle is completely beyond "natural" experience, lovingly unbounded in the present; intelligently, profusely unbounded.

BROTHER DAVID STEINDL-RAST

The simplest way of putting my experience of God would be

as a great aliveness on all levels, a kind of higher frequency of oscillation. The body feels more alive. My inner state is one of great wakefulness, mindfulness, and aliveness. Paradoxically, at the same time there is a self-forgetfulness; I get absorbed in whatever I'm looking at and become less aware of myself. There is a sense of expansion and fusion with whatever I'm with. I feel my heart expand and embrace everything there is.

CHARLES TART

One way to describe my experience of God is that at its best it's a feeling of spaciousness through which I realize that most of my life is very cramped. Normally, I'm rushing from one thing to the next in a forced kind of way. When I feel in touch with the Greater, it feels as if there is time to appreciate what is, and to draw on a calmer, deeper level of myself. When I'm in that kind of spacious state, my body feels calm, and that seems to be the way the body should be naturally.

MARIANNE WILLIAMSON

For me, the experience of God means the experience of a very deep peace. I think we all crave mental stillness at this point. We need to drop the chatter, even transformational chatter. Sometimes, people ask me how to know what God is saying to them, as though His voice would have a certain tenor or something. But the voice for God is a small, still voice. We can only hear it when the mind is quiet.

"God deliver us from sullen saints."
ST. TERESA OF AVILA

3

Diving Into the Divine

*"I was drowning in the deeps of the ocean of
this world and thou didst save me. Thou
hast united thy heart to my heart."*
KABIR

Throughout history, people have used countless methods of
experiencing the Divine. Some involve hurting one's body,
such as lying on a bed of nails or ingesting dangerous drugs.
Other methods involve doing absolutely nothing, such as
waiting for God's grace to descend. In particular religious traditions, certain techniques are emphasized. In Judaism, for
instance, study and contemplation of the Torah is encouraged, while in certain sects of Buddhism, meditation is considered the cornerstone of deepening one's experience of the
"Buddha Nature."

I like to think that everyone has a combination-type lock on his or her own heart and soul. Our mission, should we decide to accept it, is to figure out the combination to that lock. Trying just one technique is like trying one set of numbers on a combination lock: while it may open the lock, the chances of success are low. The more approaches we try, the more likely it is that we'll find the magic combination that opens the door to a much deeper experience of God. In addition, the more paths we know to the "kingdom of heaven within," the more opportunities we have for diving into the divine.

In my own case, since I felt that I wasn't getting anywhere on my own, a spiritual teacher had to tell me what would be helpful to try. He told me to sing devotional songs to God—a practice I thought was "beneath me." As a highly intellectual person, I viewed the idea of singing songs to God as very embarrassing. Lo and behold, around the third or fourth time I tried, I was suddenly overwhelmed with feelings of love, bliss, and joy! This experience taught me that I don't always know what's best for me. Nowadays, people can't stop me from singing.

The question of how to deepen one's experience of God elicits a wide variety of answers. Enjoy experimenting with the many unique suggestions offered. As with other aspects of our lives, we can get into ruts in our relationship with God. Once something works, we often go on repeating it, even though it fails to bring the experience and spirit it once did. By trying a variety of methods, you may find your connection to God is reawakened in exciting ways.

*How do you deepen your
experience of God?*

LYNN ANDREWS

To deepen my experience of God, I take time to listen. I listen to the wind, I listen to the birds, I listen to the sacred. I open up to feeling humble. I open to feeling the magic of life. I'm just in awe of the radiance of life that surrounds us every day.

I think we deepen our connection to Spirit when we remember who we really are. We are the God or Goddess self, incarnate into this lifetime. We need to develop a new vision of life. We need to remember that there's a reason for all our pain and struggle. We're here in this schoolhouse called Earth to find our path toward enlightenment. When I remember who I really am, that deepens my experience of God.

MARILYN ATTEBERRY

One way I deepen my experience of God is simply by serving others; supporting people to love themselves no matter what as they accept their feelings and thoughts and desires. Putting myself in situations in which people commit to living a life of purpose, empowering thought, and honest compassion always rubs off on me! Another way I deepen my experience of God is to do what I'm doing now: think, write, and talk about how blessed my life is and how grateful I am to be alive.

Right now, I'm sitting next to my son. He's conquered his disease and lives his own life. We seldom see eye-to-eye and I breathe a lot when we're together. In fact, I breathe a lot just thinking about him. Yet, I look at him now, and my experience of God deepens. I kiss my husband and go directly to God. Mozart works, too, and simply being silent.

PAT BOONE

Adoration. Praise and thanksgiving often overlap, though giving thanks to God is different from praising Him in that the act of thanking usually arises from something specific God has already done for us. I like to begin my day by spending some time telling God how I feel about Him. I really love Him! He knows it, but we both feel it's important that I express it in fresh and honest ways. Jesus actually urges us to be more like children in our response to God. And often, the more childlike and unsophisticated we can become during these periods of adoration, the more likely we are to please God and get ourselves into a spiritually sensitive mood that will help us discern His will.

Because my friendship with God is a real and living one, and because I have come to believe that I'm never out of His presence, I often start a conversation with Him before I even get out of bed. Usually, when I first open my eyes and realize that I'm awake, I'll just thank the Lord for a new day, for my health or for any other blessings that come to mind. Sometimes, I'll just say, "Good morning, Lord!" the very first thing. Right away, I'm aware of Someone on the other end of the line, and my perspective and priorities are set in order almost automatically. Speaking with Him from then on throughout the day seems natural and easy, as with any other friend.

JOAN BORYSENKO

For me, getting into the present—what's been called "mindfulness"—is largely a process of being grateful. When I get up in the morning, I look around and feel grateful for the mountains in the distance. I feel grateful for the sun shining, or the snow falling. I feel grateful for having eyes to see. If we practice gratitude, then being in the present moment (mindfulness) follows directly from that. Grace is also very important. Divine grace is there all around us. Helpful beings and spirits are all around us. When our desire to be in God's presence is really authentic, when we express that in our thoughts (which are, in fact, prayers), then we get a great deal of help. I think desire and intention are the two magic ingredients for experiencing Grace.

LEVAR BURTON

Right now, I am totally energized around my work—what I consider my destiny path. As I write and direct these days, I feel so much in alignment with my life's purpose. When I came into this body, I made an agreement to do specific work along the lines of waking up humanity to the truth of our spiritual journey. When I am engaged in that process, I strongly feel the presence of God in me and working through me.

DEEPAK CHOPRA

It is important to talk about love, to think about it, to seek it out, and to encourage it. To put this in the form of an exercise, make a commitment to yourself to do the following:

1. Think about love. Take time to recall the love you shared with your parents, the times you expressed love to your siblings and friends. Dwell upon what is most lovable about the person who is most loving in your life today. Read deeply the poetry of love, such as is found in Shakespeare's sonnets, and the scriptures of love, such as that contained in the New Testament or in the devotional hymns of the Rig Veda.

2. Talk about love. Express your feelings directly to someone you love. If you cannot do it verbally, write a letter or a poem. You don't have to send it; the exercise is for you, to stimulate the state of love in every cell.

3. Seek out love. This is possible in many ways. Intimacy in our society is closely identified with sexual encounters, but it is an act of love to give help to the homeless and the

sick, to deliver a sincere compliment, or to write a note of thanks and praise.

ALAN COHEN

I deepen my experience of God by allowing time and space for what truly brings meaning to me. One of the things I've done over the last few years is to extricate myself from a lot of office work. I used to be in the office five to seven days a week, and now it's down to three days. I'm writing, I'm playing, I'm relaxing, I'm hiking, I'm swimming, I'm doing things on the beach. I have rewarding relationships. Rather than drowning out God's voice by a lot of things that are not meaningful, I make space for God to be with me.

I also make a point of following the voice of Spirit. The voice of Spirit is peaceful, it's enlivening, it's empowering, it's creative; it feels like, "Yes, this is something I can live with." I want to wake up in the morning to follow that voice, for it brings a sense of freedom and lightness. The voice of fear is always asking you to exert more control to protect yourself—it makes you feel separate. It feels gunky. After awhile, following the voice of Spirit becomes automatic. It's like riding a bike. You don't think, "I'm going to lean first to the left and then to the right." After awhile, you just know how to do it.

STAN DALE

To deepen my experience of God, I tune into myself, and I tune into my own heart. It's like putting a set of ears to my heart. When I speak, I imagine putting a set of lips to my heart because the heart is the representation of where God lives. If I'm feeling upset, I'll take a deep breath. Then I'll clarify the "static" that's going on. This helps me soften again and come from God.

RAM DASS

Deepening the experience of God can be approached in different ways. It seems to me you can lead with your mind, your emotions, or your body, but they'll all eventually bring you to the same place. The other parts will follow afterward. When I lead with my mind, I engage in a practice that deepens my concentration and my awareness of what is happening from moment to moment. Meditation is an example of this. When I lead with my body or energy system, I do pranayama (breath exercises) combined with hatha yoga and diet. Engaging in these practices helps awaken the kundalini that forces you into other planes of consciousness. Experiencing these other states of consciousness increases my appreciation of God because it puts in perspective the state of mind I started from. Ultimately, these practices can assist me in entering into an absolute reality in which I merge with God.

There are a couple of approaches to the emotional path. One is the practice of gratitude. Gratitude opens your heart, and opening your heart is a wonderful and easy way for God to slip in. I think that humor, love, and gratitude are truly wonderful vehicles for preparing a being to experience God. They soften your paranoia, your resistance, and your doubt. In the practice of gratitude, you express gratefulness for being allowed to be backstage to enjoy the production known as *your life*. You get to be the creator as well as the audience and actors. The practice of gratitude can also show you all the holdings of your mind. What you can't feel grateful for soon becomes apparent, and those are simply the things you can't see the wisdom behind.

The other emotional path is one in which you start with somebody you absolutely love, such as Krishna or Christ, and you sing to, praise, read poetry about, and basically open your heart to this person in an almost romantic way. I've just come from an all-night chanting session where we sang to our Beloved. At some point you reach a state where all your emotions are present, the mind becomes very quiet, and your body's energies start to move. As I mentioned before, you can lead with one system, and the others will soon follow.

BRUCE DAVIS

Everybody has an image of God that touches them, whether it's Jesus, Mary, one's own kids, a teacher, or nature. I think it's very important to spend time with that form and really open your heart to it. After all, the first commandment is "Thou shalt love the Lord thy God with all thy heart, with all thy mind, with all thy soul, and with all thy strength." For me, I go to Mass every day and take the Eucharist, and I pray and I meditate. I find the world's religions really nourish me. I don't get caught up in the politics and the personality of a particular religion. It's the essence of the religions that matter, and when you remove the veneer like the language, they all basically speak about the same thing.

WAYNE DYER

I deepen my experience of God by banishing doubt. I'm convinced that there's more to life than just this form and the physical universe. This body is just like a garage where you park your soul for a brief period of time. Our lives are like parentheses in eternity.

The other thing I do is be the witness, the observer. In order to get into the witness self, you need to get beyond two things: your body and your mind. First, you need to get beyond your body. We do this all the time. After all, we're not sitting here beating our hearts and digesting our food; these things just happen, and we simply trust that they'll continue to happen. To get beyond your mind, you have to be able to just watch it, just as you might observe your own body. Watching my thoughts come and go deepens my experience.

WARREN FARRELL

Spending time in the mountains, forests, or being alone helps me to deepen the experience of God. Such things get me away from thoughts like "I need to make a phone call at eight o'clock, then I have an appointment at nine," etc. It takes me away from the minutia and allows me to feel the larger picture and get a perspective on the game of life.

When I feel very loved or loving, or when I nurture and support other people, my experience is deepened. Such things help me to feel connected to a larger purpose and meaning. It makes me feel warm inside.

WILLIS HARMAN

My experience of God deepens itself when I am not trying to deepen it. To remember to attend to it feels important; to attempt to do anything more than simply accept it seems to get in the way.

RICHARD HATCH

When I surrender totally and release all my judgments and belief systems about who and what I deem God to be, I open a space to more fully receive all that is truly of God. My whole life has been a journey to unblock and free myself, to more fully allow God to express divinity through me. In doing so, I've had to face my every fear and self-worth issue. In the process, I've discovered that every aspect of my being, both good and bad, is a part of the whole. When I embrace and forgive the parts of me I judge to be negative, I find that these aspects are just wayward children left out in the cold too long. They're not really bad, just frustrated and angry that they have been unable to express themselves. The pain and trauma of abuse caused me to abandon and judge myself harshly. When

I have had the courage to stop running from myself and face my greatest fears and denials, I have walked through the doorway of disillusionment, embraced my true self, and come home to God.

LOUISE HAY

I deepen my experience of God by keeping my conscious thoughts aware of the presence of God in everyone I meet. When I can go beyond appearance, beyond behavior, and allow myself to see the true essence of a person, then I know I am connected with the Power that created me. God, the Life Force, is my breath, my heartbeat, my joy, and my ability to think and feel. I do not have to go to a certain building or sit in a certain position to feel connected to God. God is everywhere and in everything. I am very grateful to be part of God's world.

JERRY JAMPOLSKY

I think there is a major difference between being "sort of committed" and being *totally* committed. Currently, I get up at 4:30 A.M., and the first thing my partner and spouse Diane Cirincione and I do is say a prayer from *A Course in Miracles*: "I'm not a body. I am free. I am still as God created me. I want the peace of God. The peace of God is everything that I want." What that prayer does for us at the beginning of a day is get us going in a direction that is right for us. Then, while still in bed, we think of people we've been in contact with recently and put them in the Light. We send love to them, and we express gratitude for the blessings we've received from the Source of all creation. Next, we go do about 45 minutes of stretching as well as a 40-minute silent nature walk together. Finally, we arrive back at the house and meditate for about

20 minutes. That's how we start each day. Of course, all this takes a fair amount of time, but it's something we cherish. If we don't do it, or we get too busy, that day simply doesn't go the same way.

Another thing we do that deepens our experience of God is to work with children and adults with life-threatening challenges. Being with such people is a very powerful lesson. It helps us detach ourselves from our bodies and realize that we are really spiritual beings that are connected forever.

GURUCHARAN SINGH KHALSA

I deepen my connection to God in the four classic ways of Yoga. The first one is called *Bana*. Bana means "a form." More specifically, it refers to the attainment of a position or form that represents the Infinite in the material plane. One aspect of Bana is the way I dress. My clothes are simple; I wear all white. These (Sikh) clothes were designed by Guru Govin Singh as a beautiful way to dress. I also refrain from cutting my hair, in effect saying "Let me be as God made me. If God gives me long hair, I'll have long hair." Let me not presume that there's been a mistake and I have to cut it away.

A second way I have of connecting with God is through *Bani*. Bani refers to the way one speaks. It recognizes the creative power of the spoken word. The Bible says, "In the beginning was the Word." By speaking from your heart, you can gain a sense of passion and understanding of your Self. It can help you to embrace the infinite. Bani is the ability to entwine your conversations with the power and precision of God's Word. One could say the opposite of Bani is gossip—idle, trivial chitchat.

A third way I deepen my contact with God is through *Seva*. Seva means selfless service. It is a form of service based on being in the moment, when you simply act as the hands of

God. When I become aware of such opportunities, I try to take them. And last, there's *Simran*. Simran pretty much means meditation on the names of God. For me, Simran is a constant practice. It eventually becomes a subconscious habit that is going on all the time. It's repeating the names (mantras) of God—but without conscious effort.

THE DALAI LAMA

When I meet new people, in my mind there is no barrier, no curtain. As human beings you are my brothers and sisters; there is no difference in substance. I can talk with you as I would to old friends. With this feeling we can communicate without any difficulty and can make heart-to-heart contact. Based on such genuine human relations—real feeling for each other, understanding each other—we can develop mutual trust and respect. From that, we can share other people's suffering and build harmony in human society.

KENNY LOGGINS

To feel is to communicate with your Spirit—with God. Feeling is God's mirror; intuition is God's telephone. To seek your truth is to deepen your connection to Spirit.

EMMETT MILLER

Usually, a competing event or demand is going on at the time I become aware of the divine presence. I deepen my experience by stopping and honoring it. I'm reminded of an old Italian movie I saw about a playboy-type lover who was able to function sexually only when a woman's husband was knocking on the door saying, "Are you in there?" That is the only moment he would get turned on. Sometimes experiencing the divine feels like that to me. It's often in the most inopportune moments that I become aware of the divine presence. It's as if some part of me is always guarding against it, but during inopportune moments, that part of me drops away and I have to make a choice as to whether or not to focus on it. I have to make an effort to stand up for it.

DAN MILLMAN

If I try to deepen the experience of God, I become addicted to it, in the sense that whatever I was feeling just prior to wanting to deepen it wasn't enough, and this brings me "down." I just let it happen as it happens and don't try to deepen it—although I suppose I tend to feel it when I let go of whatever else is going on, and open my eyes and feelings to what I call the bigger picture of life (or the transcendent reality, or to my higher self). That can happen in meditation, or spontaneously, in the form of unreasonable happiness while sitting under a tree.

PAM OSLIE

Being still is a way of deepening one's experience of God. I also read books, I hear other people's ideas of God, and I keep reminding myself of that connection. I practice meditation. Meditation to me is not sitting in a corner and chanting; it's being still. I often have a dialogue with God, which helps me become aware of that presence.

M. SCOTT PECK

My two hours doing nothing are the most important hours of the day for me. I do not take them all in one gulp. Usually, they are distributed into three forty-minute periods: shortly after I first awaken, in the late afternoon, and again before I sleep. They are "alone" times, times of quiet and solitude. I could not survive without them.

I refer to these periods as my "prayer time." During them I actually spend no more than five to ten percent of the time in what most people would call prayer: talking to God. And no more than five to ten percent in meditation: listening for God. Ninety percent of the time I'm just thinking.

One of the things I am continually doing during my prayer time is checking out my life with my Ideal Observer. "Tell me, God," I am asking, "what I just did or what I am thinking of doing—how does it look through your eyes? Does it look civil?"

PETER RUSSELL

I open up to my preferred state of being when I practice forgiveness and compassion. I think what makes our hearts hard are the attitudes and judgments we hold against other people. They could be good judgments or bad—it doesn't matter. Either way, judgments are a way of categorizing people, of putting them in a box. By doing that, we're not really open to seeing a person as another conscious entity. The act of stepping beyond judgments and seeing others as they really are opens the heart. For me, that's the essence of forgiveness and the beginning of true compassion.

BERNIE SIEGEL

I think what has deepened my experience of God had to do with my parents' message to me that every event was something that God was participating in. When your child has cancer you can say, "Oh, why me, why did God give my child cancer?" Or you can say, "What do we do with what God has given us?" The Biblical line in Job is "Afflictions heal and adversity opens you to a new reality." So how do I deepen my experience of God? Through afflictions and adversity. The

Talmud tells us, "He who rejoices in the afflictions that are brought upon the self brings salvation to the world." I think it's hard to deepen your experience when nothing goes wrong.

The crazy thing is that things are always going wrong. Even if you interview lottery winners, they'll tell you winning millions made a mess out of their lives. So in a sense everything is adverse and can be used to deepen your relationship with God. Each experience helps you learn new ways to love the world unconditionally.

BROTHER DAVID STEINDL-RAST

Well, I've found that I cannot aim head-on for a deepening of my experience of God, it always comes as a complete gift, usually as a surprise, in situations where I least expect it. It's often triggered by very small and insignificant things. It may happen while waiting in a dentist's office or being stuck in rush-hour traffic. It can happen at any moment. But I prepare myself by cultivating gratefulness in my life, because that puts me into the present moment and opens me. Somehow, gratefulness seems to be a key for me, because, if I take things for granted, they're hardly registered. Gratefulness and mindfulness are almost synonymous except that their emphasis is a little different. In mindfulness, the emphasis is more on the thought, in gratefulness, the emphasis is more on the heart.

CHARLES TART

I no longer try to deepen my experience. If I try (and I have done too often), my rigid superego comes in and says, "Well, this is a little improvement, but it's not good enough. You know, if you're going to experience something it should be at least as good as a psychedelic experience." Of course, these thoughts get me lost in concepts again, which lessen whatev-

er experience I was having. So I let go of the ridiculous stan-
dards my superego has and just try to be with what's in the
moment. Sometimes it seems to go deeper, and sometimes it
doesn't, but that's what is.

MARIANNE WILLIAMSON

I deepen my experience of God through prayer, meditation
and forgiveness. I try to remember that everything can be an
experience of God, because God is in my mind.

I practice *A Course In Miracles* which trains my mind to perceive other people's innocence, rather than their guilt. It's certainly not always easy, but it's clearly the way to find peace in
this world.

"Blessed is he who does good to others and
desires not that others should do good to him."
BROTHER GILES

4

How I Pray or Meditate

*"Prayer does not change God, but it changes
him who prays."*
KIERKEGAARD

Newsweek reported in 1992 that 88 percent of Americans pray
and/or meditate. Yet only 26 percent say they consistently
feel God's presence when doing so, and a full 21 percent of
people who pray or meditate say they have never felt God's
presence. If you assume that God is equally available to all
people, then why do some folks consistently feel His presence
while others do not? Is there anything we can do to more
deeply connect with God when we meditate or pray?

In the answers that follow, the experts gave us several different methods of meditation and prayer. Often, the respondents talked about their *beliefs* concerning meditation and

prayer more than they did about the actual techniques they use. Perhaps our beliefs about God and about these practices have a major impact on the experience we have. Indeed, there's scientific evidence to support this idea. In his book, *Beyond the Relaxation Response,* Harvard physician Herbert Bensen explains that a person's level of faith clearly affects the degree of physiological changes that occur during meditation and prayer. In other words, one's degree of faith in a technique is just as important as the technique itself.

What are the critical factors that help people to have more intimate contact with God? In the answers that follow, perhaps some new ways of connecting with God's presence will spark your interest (and rekindle your interest in meditation and prayer).

When you meditate and/or pray, how do you connect with the Divine Presence?

LYNN ANDREWS

To connect to my center, in my mind I perform a ritual in which I circle around to the four directions. The South represents the little girl within me as well as my understanding of substance. The West represents where my emotions live and my adolescent self. The North is symbolic of my spirit, my strength, and my adult self. Finally, I imagine moving to the East, which represents wisdom and intellect. I move for a moment into each of these four sacred caves and check how it feels. Then I move into the center of my circle, which is the position of the Self, and I just sit inside myself in that place of dominion. Sometimes, rather than just doing it in my mind,

I'll actually move my body in each of these directions.

I also have a deck of cards called "The Power Deck." The Power Deck was given to me through the Sisterhood of the Shields. It's basically a teaching deck; it's not a Tarot deck at all. It has beautiful aspects of nature on one side of each card, with a reading on the opposite side that goes along with the painting. The words usually have to do with taking your power and standing in the center of your being. Using this set of cards reminds me of my sense of Godliness. As I draw a card and read it, I'll move around my "inner circle," and then I'll look at the card as I move into a place the card represents. I use the cards a lot in order to move back to my center. When you're living in a city in the twentieth century, you need all the help you can get. I recommend it for people who want to stay centered in their sense of sacredness, yet don't have the time to perform a full ceremony in nature.

PAT BOONE

Though prayer does have its supernatural aspects, I really believe that the technique is as simple as discussion with another human being, with the head tilted slightly upward. Clement of Alexandria once referred to prayer as "conversation" with God, and I think he nailed it! That's probably the best definition you'll ever come across.

If you want to learn how to pray effectively, go sit quietly in the country for a few hours, outside the clanging noise of civilization. Without any of the usual urban distractions, try listening to the voices of the woods and waters and animals around you. These individual cries and movements in the natural world have always seemed to me to be part of the universal communication between the Creator and His creation—in just the way that the cooing and happy gurgling of a little baby sparks joy in the heart of its proud parent. The song of an individual bird or the soothing sound of a quiet brook will reach out and encompass you and, I believe, lift you into a spiritual sensitivity beyond the physical world. A lot of the natural sound of nature is pure joy, spontaneous exultation, uninhibited praise for a Creator/God, for life itself!

You don't have to learn some special prayer jargon to start a conversation with God. Honesty and a willingness to establish a personal relationship with Him are the only initial requirements. God is looking for an opportunity to reveal Himself to you, so if you put Him to the test and then watch for an answer without too many preconceptions about how that answer will come, I can guarantee you that you'll be in for some exciting surprises.

It's the same situation that any father finds himself in when his infant begins to reach out to him, begins to recognize him, to laugh with delight when he sees his father's face—the reaching out of those little, stubby, dimpled hands is absolutely irresistible to the proud father! The baby's attempt at communication may be limited and inadequate, but the father is delighted with the attempt and will work with this child to develop and broaden the possibilities of their communication and their ongoing relationship. God is just·like that.

JOAN BORYSENKO

Sometimes when I meditate and pray I feel as if the only thing I've connected up with is my own complaining, doubting, noisy mind. This is especially true if I'm really preoccupied by something. In such cases, I like to center myself by doing a moving meditation like hatha yoga. That focuses my mind.

Yet my very favorite way of connecting with God's presence involves three practices. First, I do an invocation of the angels from mystical Judaism. Then I say the Unity Church prayer of protection. Finally, I say Buddhist *metta*, or loving kindness blessings. This hybrid practice culminates in absorption in the Divine Presence.

In case you want to invoke the angels, you should know that it's very easy. You just call them, and there they are. Ask for Michael's presence on your right; he is the angel of love. Ask for his help where your own love fails. Gabriel is on your left—the angel of strength and courage, who is very helpful in overcoming fear. Call for Uriel in front of you—the angel of Clear Mind, or right discrimination. Raphael, the angel of healing, is in back of you. I like to invite him into my body and perceptions. Finally, I call upon the Shekina, the feminine aspect of God in mystical Judaism—that part of the Divine that dwells within us and all creation. I feel Her Presence flooding me from above and from within. And then I sit with that. It's a great meditation, and once you know the presence of the angels you can call on them throughout the day and night!

DEEPAK CHOPRA

Transcendental Meditation is based on the silent repetition of a specific Sanskrit word, or mantra, whose sound vibrations gradually lead the mind out of its normal thinking process and into the silence that underlies thought. As such, a mantra is a very specific message inserted into the nervous system.

ALAN COHEN

To pray or meditate I take images that inspire me. I take such words as the 23rd Psalm or the Lord's Prayer, and I call forth my vision of a master soul or an angel. I work with light, drawing light into my body and magnifying it. I imagine a great vortex of light over my head and then invite it down into my being. I visualize it moving into different parts of my body, emotions, and thoughts. I imagine a healing temple; it's a chapel in nature, and I take people to it in some guided meditations.

Sometimes I take an inspiring phrase from the Bible, or a prayer, and work with that, slipping it into the deeper levels of my being. I let it settle down into the very fabric of myself. I might, for example, use the phrase, "My grace is sufficient unto thee," which is something that Jesus said. I repeat it while relaxing my mind which wants to judge and evaluate, and I link up with the Higher Mind that said it. It's like sending a pipeline into the Source of such a phrase.

Many people just mouth the words in a rote, parrot-like way. They don't really think about them; they're just doing their duty. Instead, we can send a pipeline into the very Source from which the author got the words. Sometimes, when I teach the Lord's Prayer in a meditation class, I feel as if it is coming through me just as it came through Jesus. I know exactly what he knew, and we're both coming from the same Source. I repeat the words slowly several times to myself. "My grace is sufficient unto thee." "My grace is sufficient unto thee." And then I use images in my daily life that pop up at times when I'm not recognizing or accepting grace, and I just apply that phrase, "My grace is sufficient." Prayer is contemplating the facts of life from the highest point of view.

RAM DASS

When I meditate, I use two Buddhist practices. In the first, I focus on a muscle in my abdomen as it rises and falls with my breath. I just bring my full awareness to my abdomen, and every time my mind wanders I draw it back to that place. Eventually, my mind gets very concentrated, and at that point deeper processes open up. The other technique I use is a practice of turning in on my own awareness. It's like a flashlight looking at itself, a form of Ramana Maharshi's technique of asking, "Who am I?" But instead of doing it in an analytic, thoughtful way, I use statements like "rest your weary mind, and let everything be as it is." It's a way of letting go of one's sense of "somebodyness." It's an advanced practice in which you keep identifying back and back to just pure awareness.

In praying when I'm about to have a meal, I offer it to my guru, even though he's not embodied anymore. In a way, I really offer it to the deepest truth of what I am, and I just use my guru as a form that I can imagine. So I offer him the food and wait while he takes the essence of it, and then after "he" offers it back, it becomes consecrated food—and I begin eating. I think of it as a way to eat the leftovers of God. Any time before I eat, I wait until I experience that process.

BRUCE DAVIS

Remember that God's presence is our presence, and it's only our thoughts and pictures that put a block in the ocean that's already inside of us. So most people try to connect with something, but that's an illusion; it's our own energy, our own presence that we connect with. As I practice sitting, my thoughts block me less, and I just feel this big expansive Self.

In my retreats, I recommend that people experience God through devotion. I tell them to feel their devotion toward God in whatever form most touches them: nature, their kids, a teacher, whatever. Pour your heart out into the devotion, and then sit in the silence and stillness. Sitting in devotion clears out all the emotional things that are in our way. Resentments, anxieties, and fears are all just cleared away.

Devotion is the practice of making friends with emptiness. In our culture, we resist emptiness. We're always trying to fill ourselves up or stay busy and distracted. In my retreats, I help people make friends with their loneliness, make friends with their physical and financial vulnerability. I direct participants to just spend time making friends with the feelings that come up. Rather than reacting to their feelings, they watch those feelings. When you learn to do this, you eventually become less anxious. The everyday world doesn't push and pull you as much because, at your core, you've made friends with emptiness.

WAYNE DYER

One doesn't have to be sitting quietly in a room alone in order to meditate. You can become the "witness" at any time in your life. For me, to watch my thoughts and feelings come and go is meditation. I can be in a business meeting and watch my thoughts. I watch what offends me, I watch where my ego is, and I begin to detach myself from the thoughts I'm having. It's common to teach people who experience chronic pain to simply observe the pain and notice how it shows up. You can do the same thing with any thought or emotion: worry, anger, whatever comes up.

There's a wonderful quotation from Nisargadata Maharaj that says, "In my world, nothing ever goes wrong." That's a very powerful notion, because what he's saying is that all our problems are part of the body's world—and that's not *his* world. Sometimes I'll use this quotation as an affirmation. I'll think, "In my world, nothing ever goes wrong." My world is the spiritual world, and from there I can observe my body and my thoughts. I just become a witness to all of it.

WARREN FARRELL

I meditate every day, but I rarely pray, although sometimes when I'm very happy I'll say, "Thank you, God." (I guess I'm more likely to give God credit than to ask God for help.) When I meditate I just relax my entire body and imagine myself floating in a beautiful ocean in the Caribbean. Then I imagine lying down in the sand and letting the sun nurture me. This brings me to the feeling that nothing is more important in my life than the present moment and totally letting everything go. It makes me feel enormously grateful and centered.

WILLIS HARMAN

In my earlier years (I am 75 years old), I sought encounters with the Divine through meditative discipline, study, personal relationships, and nature. I believe such seeking was important, but this phase of my life seems more about finding and doing my own creative work, acting in accordance with inner guidance, "living on purpose." When I was in the "seeking" stage, I could not have imagined that life would be so simple as it now seems. The part of me that is the divine center, that knows what would be best for me to do, is never absent. I have only to attend to it, act accordingly, and observe what experience follows. All experience is feedback; not good or bad, just feedback to be learned from.

RICHARD HATCH

For me, prayer does not involve stopping what I'm doing to go inside and connect with God. Instead, it's a state of doing, expressing, and receiving that becomes a walking prayer or walking meditation. We are constantly receiving from God. If we act on what we receive, we feel a sense of empowerment. We then find ourselves moving into a rhythm of doing, dancing, singing and joyously expressing God's energy.

Once you can contact that Light inside and express it moment-to-moment in your life, you no longer need to sit, stop, and go inside. You're in alignment with God. You don't have to contact God if you're already one with God. For me, expressing God's energy through sculpting, painting, walking, or whatever method of expression is a form of prayer to God. It is fulfilling our divine mission.

LOUISE HAY

To pray I close my eyes, feel gratitude for my breath, and say, "God, I am here. What is it you want me to know?" The silence that envelopes me is alive with the power and presence of the Universe.

JERRY JAMPOLSKY

Here's a prayer I like to say before every lecture and healing work I do: "I'm here only to be truly helpful. I'm here to represent You who sent me. I do not have to worry about what to say or what to do because You who sent me will direct me. I am content to be wherever You wish, knowing that You go there with me. I will be healed as I let You teach me to heal." That's a little prayer from *A Course in Miracles*. It helps me to set my ego aside so that Spirit can take over.

GURUCHARAN SINGH KHALSA

When I meditate, the means of connecting with the Infinite is to get out of the way. If you're a flea on a dog, it makes no sense to run around all the time and try to find a dog; you're already on the dog. In the same way, looking for God is a useless act. Anyone who searches for God is a fool, because all you need to do is be quiet and God will find you. My teacher, Yogi Bhajan, once wrote in a poem, "I looked everywhere for God, and decided in the end there wasn't anything there—so I stopped looking. Then He showed up."

Some people have the idea of effortless effort—but they think that means you don't try. You do, but you try without attachment. Many people mistake detachment for non-attachment. In the Bhagavad Gita, Krishna (God) tells Arjuna he has to act and fight the battle before him. So Arjuna tries to detach from the whole experience, but Krishna says, "No, no. You don't do that. You have to act with full passion, but be non-attached to what happens." When you can do that, you align yourself to a larger conductor and become part of the greater orchestra. When I meditate, I try to get out of the way so that the "larger orchestra" can manifest through me. Instead of being one isolated instrument, I become instrumental in expressing the music of the One.

EMMETT MILLER

I begin meditation by relaxing my body deeply. I focus on relaxing the muscles in my eyelids until they don't want to stay open, and then I let the feeling of relaxation in my eyelids flow progressively throughout my body. Then I clear my mind by counting backward and letting the numbers disappear as I count down; it's like setting down a heavy suitcase. At first it took some time to do this, but with practice I've learned to set the "suitcase" of my mind down more quickly and easily. With practice, I've become better at it.

Once the quiet is there, I reflect on a recent time in which I was touched deeply by something. I go back to that experience and recreate the scene in my mind until I feel a shift in my heart. When in touch with my heart, I just follow that feeling. It's like following a golden thread back to home.

DAN MILLMAN

I do not pray in the usual sense of being a separate and mortal "me" invoking, speaking with, asking favors of, or even communing with a separate and higher Someone or Something. I just open to the feeling of the Mystery.

EDGAR MITCHELL

I try to quiet my body and mind and follow a certain feeling. If I get off-track, I return to the feeling of total peace and try to expand it once again. With prayer, what I do before I go into a deep meditative state is consciously think of outcomes I want to create. Then, when I go into the meditative state, my voiced reality (prayer) becomes part of my deepest consciousness. Doing that helps create the outcomes I desire. It's a way of taking a goal and imprinting it on Reality.

PAM OSLIE

I talk to God more often than I listen to God. I used to think that was bad. I'd think, "Why don't you just shut up and listen?" Now I don't put myself down for that any more. Since I'm not separate from God, when I talk to God it's really God expressing Itself so It can hear Itself. It's as if talking to God (prayer) and listening to God (meditation) were the same. It's all about learning that there's no separation, learning that there's just one unity.

M. SCOTT PECK

Listening for God is my definition of meditation. It is not the way, however, the word is often used. The essence of Transcendental Meditation (TM), for instance, is attentiveness to a repetitive sound—a mantra—that one says silently to oneself, and not attentiveness to God.

Far closer to true meditation, from my point of view, is the Zen Buddhist meditative practice called "No Mind." Here the practitioner is instructed not to fill the mind, as with a mantra, but to empty it. It is not an easy process. Despite the fact that mystics through the ages have extolled the virtues of emptiness, people are generally quite terrified of it. It may help to remember, therefore, that the purpose of emptying the mind is not ultimately to have nothing there; rather it is to make room in the mind for something new, something unexpected to come in. What is this something new? It is the voice of God.

PETER RUSSELL

I pray, but not in the way it's usually thought of. I don't say, "Please God, give me a car." Nor do I ask, "Please let me have guidance on what to do with my life." It's difficult for me to distinguish between true inner guidance and mere inner garbage, which comes from the ego, so my technique of prayer is my way of distinguishing between guidance and garbage. Instead of asking for guidance on what to do, I ask, "Is there a different way of perceiving this situation?" When I ask this question, it keeps my ego from coming in because the ego tells me only what to do, not how to see. The voice of God speaks in terms of a different way of seeing a situation. When I ask for that, what comes to me is a much more loving way of seeing things. It's a tremendous release.

I even use this technique when doing business transactions. Often in business, I can fall into the mode of seeing the other person as an enemy. I think "this person is trying to get more out of me than I want to give." But if I ask for another way to see the situation, I begin to see them in a much more compassionate light. In a period of just a few seconds, I can go from feeling cut off emotionally, to a wide-open loving mode. Of course, this technique is a tremendous help in my personal relationships as well.

BERNIE SIEGEL

Some people may call it prayer, some may call it meditation, but to me it's just a conversation, just a feeling that I am surrounded by a Force and energy. When I enter into difficult times or risky situations, I always say "be with me." My feeling is that God is all around. I don't have to connect; I just speak. Nor do I have to be in a special place where God is, because God IS—period. I just let my thoughts out, and they become one with God.

Generally, I speak internally to God, and I don't mind asking for favors. If I'm in an airplane, I ask God to participate in holding the plane together and making it a safe journey. I truly feel that such a prayer will help that plane make it. Now, if the plane crashes it isn't because God said, "You don't deserve to have a safe journey; you've been a bad boy, so now we'll crash your plane." Those things happen, but I truly believe that if everyone on the plane prayed, we'd have a better chance of making it than if everybody did not.

Even as a kid, I'd look up and say, "What am I supposed to do? Give me a sign. Where should I go to school?" And things would happen, and invariably I'd realize later that God was right. Everything worked out. I believe that God frequently redirects us.

BROTHER DAVID STEINDL-RAST

"Prayer" is a very wide term. It includes all sorts of things, so my prayer life includes a great variety of activities: I may chant songs, go for a walk, soak in a hot tub, read poetry, or play with my cat. The essence of prayer as I understand the term is communication with the Ultimate. I think that prayer occurs whenever someone feels, "When I do this, then I really feel as if I'm at home with the Ultimate." That's a person's starting point for developing their prayer life. That could occur from watering African violets, reading sacred scripture, playing an instrument, or any number of activities.

MARSHA SINETAR

The "how" questions—and we all have them—seem distractive, alienating, and a sly technique of the intellect designed to cut us off from a relationship with God. In fact, each of us has the potential to be totally spiritual. There is *nothing special to do*. All contemplative acts like prayer, meditation, reading scripture (which is, to me, the ingestion and assimilation of God's Word), and concrete acts like gardening, cooking oatmeal, stacking firewood, watching movies, are all prayerful if and when we are recollected. Using our essential freedom to experience the spiritual reality (which is our life in God) is "how."

Generally, Walt Whitman's comment frames my ongoing experience: "And I know that the hand of God is the elder hand of my own, and I know that the spirit of God is the eldest brother of my own, and that [all others] are my brothers and sisters. . . ."

CHARLES TART

In the meditation traditions they say you should learn to observe thought. But they almost never advise you to *begin* learning how to meditate by trying to observe thought. They suggest starting with something more concrete. For example, in the Buddhist meditation tradition, which is one of my main practices, they say to start trying to observe something like your breath. It's a very simple and concrete object. At the grossest level, am I inhaling or exhaling? What kind of body sensation goes with it? And then the main kind of meditation I practice in that tradition is simply observing the field of body sensations. Those are much more concrete than thoughts: "Here's a wave of warm sensation in my stomach, and now that's fading, and a pulsing sensation in my hand is becoming more prominent," and the like.

When I pray, I give thanks for all the blessings I've received in life, because I think I'm very lucky. I'll remind myself of a variety of things, varying from time to time, such as wanting to be of help to others, or of the importance of using the talents I have to help increase knowledge, or of how much suffering there is in the world and my hope that I can do at least a little something to lessen it. And then I usually either pray specifically for somebody else's health or welfare or to be guided in some enterprise I'm doing. I accept the fact that I'm kind of stubborn, but I pray that I'll be subtly guided to do my best and even do some good. Depending on my mood, I'll pray to different beings. If I'm in a Buddhist frame of mind, I'll think I'm praying to some Bodhisattva. Sometimes I'll pray to God; sometimes I'll think of praying to the Highest, whatever that is. I don't really know what or who I pray to, except that it's something or someone much vaster and wiser than I am.

MARIANNE WILLIAMSON

I do both Transcendental Meditation and lessons from *A Course In Miracles*. On the days I meditate, my life is different than on the days when I don't. I think we underestimate the power of words. When we get on our knees and say "God help me," the skies open. In the Bible it says, "In the beginning was the Word." It doesn't matter what sacred words we say. They can be a mantra, a prayer, anything. I think the highest level of prayer is a prayer for conscious contact, a connection with His Mind. It's not so important how we pray. What's important is that we remember to actually do it.

*"I do not pray for a lighter load, but
a stronger back."*
PHILLIP BROOKS

5

What Cuts Me Off From God

*"The safest road to hell is the gradual one—
the gentle slope, without sudden turnings,
without milestones, without signposts."*
C.S. LEWIS

The word *sin* as derived from ancient Aramaic was really an archery term that meant "to miss the mark or bullseye." A "sin" was simply anything you did that seemed to lessen your contact with God. Of course, today, sin has a more negative connotation. Yet if God could be considered the "bullseye," most of us are missing the mark almost all the time. If God is so omnipresent, how exactly do we cut ourselves off from God?

In my work as a psychotherapist, I often ask people about their relationship with God. Even for those who believe fully in God, I repeatedly see three defenses get in the way of their establishing a close and nurturing relationship with their Source. The first defense is blame. Many people blame God secretly for the difficulties in the world or in their own lives, thereby cutting themselves off from divine intimacy. The second defense is denial. People frequently deny that they lack intimacy with God, despite the fact that the last time they felt truly connected to God was many weeks, months, or even years ago. And last, there is the defense of distraction. Many people create so much drama, busyness, and activity in their lives that the notion of spending quality time with God each day seems virtually impossible. If we're not careful, the defenses of blame, denial and distraction can sneak into our own heads and eat away at our connection to our Higher Power.

In order to hit a target, it is unnecessary to know exactly where it is. One need only know all the places it is *not*. Many people in Western society have had the chance to see that the "bullseye" in life is *not* to be found in money, or relationships, or whatever other things we thought in the past would bring us lasting happiness. A "sin" is merely putting our hope for happiness exclusively in highly temporary things. As we see that such things fail to bring us lasting fulfillment, our focus naturally turns to spirituality.

By reading the various ways people lessen their contact with God, it's possible to surmise where God *can* be found. A spiritual teacher I once knew said, "You need not know where to find God. You need only stop running away from Him so vigorously. Once you stop running in the wrong direction, God will be there waiting for you. . . ."

Is there anything you do that seems to lessen your experience of God?

LYNN ANDREWS

I think what cuts most of us off from God is the pace at which we live. My teachers said a long time ago that the slower you go physically, the faster you go spiritually. And the slower you go spiritually, the faster you go physically.

Most of us are on a very interesting treadmill. The money that we have earned in the past is now worth less than we thought it would be. If we're supporting families, we have to work twice as hard as we did a few years ago to make the same amount of money. At the same time, we're losing our sense of tradition. We're even losing our sense of family. The television is constantly tearing things apart, but no alternatives are given. Maybe this loss of faith in everything around us will finally prove to be a gift. Maybe it'll finally throw us back on ourselves and our sense of the Great Spirit.

MARILYN ATTEBERRY

I lose touch with the omnipresent, omnipotent omniscience of God when I allow some illusion to become solid and appear extremely REAL. What kind of illusion? Oh, fear. Judgment. Busy-ness. Self-flagellation. Preoccupation with the mundane. Then, instead of being grateful, I worry and snap and run around in circles, or do my paralyzed pacing trick. One of my most effective ways of losing touch with God is losing something physical: keys, purse, day runner, lipstick . . . the real important things of life. And losing my sense of humor works every time!

PAT BOONE

The evidence for God is all around us, and He frequently tries to break through our overbearing self-centeredness and egotism to begin a dialogue with us; but we are simply too busy to listen. There is a war going on. And we're in the middle of it! The whole Bible, from Genesis through Revelation, is this detailed story of an all-out elemental war between God and Satan. Oh, I know, in spite of all the movies like *The Exorcist, The Omen, The Amityville Horror,* and the countless books and TV moves about demons and Satanic invasions, it's still not popular among "practical"-thinking people to admit the existence of a real devil.

Any man who decides he wants to develop a genuine relationship with God and to communicate with Him personally will meet with premeditated, highly effective, diabolic opposition! You can count on it! When a man get serious about praying, about partnership with God, he automatically becomes dangerous to God's enemy, Satan. But old Lucifer is too cunning, too experienced, to make a frontal attack, exposing who he is and his intentions for your soul. Instead, he'll just try to muddy the water, discredit the whole idea of faith and prayer, distract and confuse you, and try to get you to give the whole idea up.

JOAN BORYSENKO

At times when I'm feeling things like resentment, judgment, fear or guilt, it's very hard for me to let go into the Divine Presence. Those emotions may cut me off from God. But sometimes, right in the grips of emotions like that, I have a very powerful experience of God that completely melts those feelings. I think it's by the power of Grace. If I thought I had to have all my stuff worked out before I could feel the Divine Presence, I'd give up. It would be too big a job.

LEVAR BURTON

Fear! Boom—end of story. That's what cuts me off from God. Of course, fear can manifest in many forms. Yet the bottom line is that there is fear and there is God. What gets me into fear is my ego. I experience fear as a result of buying into the illusion that ego is in control. Whenever I start doubting the purpose in my life, I fall into the grips of fear. Whenever I buy into the illusion that my ego has to be in control, fear rushes in.

MANTAK CHIA

First, when energy is blocked, we lose our connection to God. Second, when a man ejaculates, he loses his sexual energy, and this lessens his energy available to contact God. For women, when they menstruate they lose energy, and therefore they lessen their contact with God. In Taoism, it was discovered that one's sexual energy, when activated, had the same vibration as the God force; so if this energy was wasted, it lessened the energy available to commune with God. It's important to note that sex and ejaculation are two different things. You can learn to orgasm without ejaculating, in which case you won't lose any energy. In my books, I detail ways men and women can cultivate their sexual energy and have sex without losing their vital energy through ejaculation or menstruation.

A second thing that lessens our contact with God is negative emotions. Negative emotions squeeze out or scatter your life force. With anger, you shut out your life force. In fear, you squeeze out your life force. Negative emotions lead to less energy, which in turn leaves you with too little energy to connect with God.

DEEPAK CHOPRA

It is our conditioning, our current collective world view that we were taught by our parents, teachers, and society. This way of seeing things—the old paradigm—has aptly been called "the hypnosis of social conditioning" an induced fiction in which we have collectively agreed to participate.

RAM DASS

Thinking lessens my experience of the Divine. Fascination with thought or sensation cuts me off from God. The minute awareness gets identified with anything, I have immediately cast myself into a finite prison of separateness. As I see it, the art is to be fully present with all the stuff of life but to be free of clinging to any of it.

If you ask why we identify with anything, I'd say that identification with anything is rooted in fear. To go back even further, fear is rooted in the ignorance in which we have identified ourselves as a separate entity. As long as we think we're separate, we'll feel vulnerable and afraid, and we'll have a strong desire to make ourselves feel safe, secure, and loved. Anything that intensifies one's feelings of separation from God will create more fear, which in turn creates more separation from God.

WAYNE DYER

The ego gets in the way of experiencing the Divine. The ego is nothing more than our belief in our own separateness. We're trained to think we have to be bigger than, smarter than, or make more than others. And you can't die! Death is a very embarrassing event for the ego. The ego constantly reminds us of how important we are—that we're right and others are wrong. When being guided by the ego, we feel separate.

WARREN FARRELL

Most things I do cut me off from God. What cuts me off the

most is getting too caught up in details, or getting petty or critical about something. When I lose my larger sense of supporting people to be their best, I lessen my contact with the God inside me.

LOUISE HAY

When I fail to cooperate with the Laws of Life or lose trust in them, things seem to go wrong. I will often jump into my mistrusting human mode and think that I have to take charge and be in control of everything. The Universe waits in smiling repose until I get over that. Gratitude brings me back quickly.

JERRY JAMPOLSKY

It's hard to feel God's peace for two seconds in a row, much less two days in a row. I think experiencing God is always a challenge as long as we're in a body. We have a tendency to think that the truth is simply what our eyes and ears tells us, even though there is a deeper reality. For me, I notice that any time I try to classify someone as guilty or innocent, that takes my peace of mind away. Holding onto grievances and not forgiving keeps me distant from my Source. It makes me get stuck in the past or future, and God is never in any place but the present.

GURUCHARAN SINGH KHALSA

The classic list in Yoga is greed, pride, attachment, envy, and lust. Yet, people face different challenges or blocks in different stages of the spiritual path. In the beginning stages of the path, for example, seekers face the possibility of succumbing to boredom. Such seekers must practice diligence to make sure they stay connected to God. In other stages, it's easy to get trapped by the love of power, sensuality, or pride. In more advanced stages, rather than letting go into the final surrender, you can get attached to your own happiness and holiness.

THE DALAI LAMA

The real troublemakers are anger, jealousy, impatience, and hatred. With them problems cannot be solved. Though we may have temporary success, ultimately our hatred or anger will create further difficulties. Anger makes for swift solutions. Yet, when we face problems with compassion, sincerity, and good motivation, our solutions may take longer, but ultimately they are better.

EMMETT MILLER

When I do too many things at the same time, or when I allow my life to become more complicated than is healthy for me, I lose my connection. Sometimes I'll begin to believe that some disaster can happen in my life in which I won't be able to recover, and therefore I have to defend myself against it. This creates the feeling that I have to be excessively in control, because it's not okay to surrender. When fear gets beyond a certain point like that, I feel cut off.

DAN MILLMAN

Most everything I tend to do seems to lessen or cut off the experience of God!—thinking, acting, concentrating, contracting, being a "somebody," getting lost in the details of life, putting my attention in my mind, my ego, my separate-sense.

PETER RUSSELL

What draws me off is a single belief we've been hypnotized by society to believe. In essence, this false belief states that "if you're not at peace, then you need to change the world around you to feel better." We might think we need to get some new possessions, have some new experience, or get someone to behave differently. It's all based on thinking our inner peace is dependent upon something outside us. Now, that may be true if you're hungry or very cold, but most of us are not in that position. If we're not at peace, it's because there's something internal that needs attending to. This one belief keeps us in a material mode of consciousness, worrying about the future and missing the present moment.

In a way, it's a big cosmic joke. In trying to become more satisfied, we're so worried about securing peace in the future that we lose the peace of the present moment! We can go through our entire lives worrying about our future happiness and totally miss where true peace lives—right here, right now. I find that when I engage in the world, such as reading a newspaper, watching TV, driving through traffic—whatever, the belief that runs our society begins to affect me. I begin to be drawn back into the mode of thinking that says "I need to achieve things or have things in order to be at peace."

I think that an important part of the spiritual journey is learning to live in the material world while managing to stay at peace. In the sixties, I studied Transcendental Meditation in the Himalayas with Maharishi (Mahesh Yogi). I remember that one day he told us, "You can sit here isolated from the world and do all this meditation and experience enlightenment. Yet the true test of enlightenment is whether you can experience enlightenment while standing in Times Square." And of course, I can't.

I've also noticed that if I feel fatigued, my mind tends to go into a survival mode of consciousness—and that's incompatible with the experience of God. In addition, I've noticed that after eating meat, my mind becomes more dull. Conversely, I've noticed that when I eat a lot of raw fruits and vegetables, my mind is clearer and much more in contact with my preferred state of consciousness.

BROTHER DAVID STEINDL-RAST

Anything that diminishes mindfulness lessons my experience of God. What diminishes mindfulness? Preoccupation with the self, self-pity, busyness. Activities can be like a whirlpool. They can draw me deeper and deeper into them. If I can stay on top of it all, it's fine, but too much activity can draw me into itself to such an extent that I get totally caught up in it.

For encountering the Divine, it's necessary to be present with where you are. So basically there are only three possibilities for missing it. First, there is impatience. Impatience is being ahead of yourself—which means you're no longer in the present moment. Second, there is clinging to something in the past. When we do this, the energy to be in the present is squandered. And the third possibility is to be asleep. I don't mean asleep in the literal sense but rather stupefied or sad. In the Catholic tradition, sadness is one of the main obstacles towards encounter with God. Sadness can prevent us from rising to the occasion—like a cake that doesn't rise.

BERNIE SIEGEL

Being human—I mean that can lessen the experience of the Divine. Or when ten different things go wrong. If I'm trying to call to help in different situations and nobody's at any of the phones I'm calling, after awhile it gets frustrating. I'd say that part of me separates me from God because if I really had it together I'd say, "What is God telling me?" My mother would have said, "Honey, you're being redirected; why are you getting upset? There may be something else you need to do today."

When I stop listening to my own messages and get caught

up in time and what "should" happen and what *I* want to do today, then I lose it. I always mention to people that in heaven the clocks have all the hands broken off, and on them is printed "one, two, three, four, who cares?"

MARSHA SINETAR

When I'm self-conscious or, say, reactive (with facets of unconsciousness), this slices into pure self-awareness. Then it's easy to feel separated. When I imagine that I must climb some legalistic, spiritual ladder of effort — you know, earn my way into God's graces, struggle to perfect myself (as if that were even possible) — then it's easy to get "cut off," as you say.

CHARLES TART

Fear, anger, you know, the usual human emotions. It's those that make me forget my belief that our ordinary identity is only the tip of something much vaster. They make me get caught up in the specifics of my particular identity. I think such things are so persistent because we have physical bodies we need to take care of. Our bodies are vulnerable to sickness, death, and suffering, and we have to watch out for them in this world. It's easy to get totally caught up in that and forget that our bodies are not all of what we are, even if they are an important part of what we are now.

MARIANNE WILLIAMSON

I cut myself off from God by perceiving guilt in someone. That's the essence of separation from God.

✳ ✳

*"I have only three enemies. My favorite
enemy, the one most easily influenced for the
better, is the British Empire. My second
enemy, the Indian people, is far more difficult.
But my most formidable opponent is a man
named Mohandas K Gandhi. With him I
seem to have very little influence."*
MAHATMA GANDHI

𝕲
Helpful Beliefs I Have

*"God is like a vast ocean of love, and the
Milky Way galaxy is but a speck of foam
floating in that ocean."*
RUMI

Everyone has beliefs about God—even an atheist who believes
God doesn't exist. A belief, as I mentioned before, is a feeling
of certainty about something. Basically, religions are orga-
nized groups of people who have similar beliefs about God.
Of course, since there are literally thousands of religions, there
are thousands of (often contradictory) beliefs about God.

By phrasing this question, "What beliefs have helped you
to attain a better relationship with God?" I attempted to steer
clear of having the contributors proclaim "correct" or "truth-
ful" beliefs about God. How can any of us really know what

is true about God? We can, however, reflect on the beliefs we *have* about God and whether or not they have helped us develop a better relationship with the Higher Power. If a certain way of thinking about God is highly useful to one person, then perhaps it will be useful to others.

I didn't realize how limited my conception of God was until I heard people express beliefs I had never even conceived of. I have occasionally "tried on a new belief " to see if it "fit." If it felt as if it deepened my connection to God, I incorporated it into my own belief system. You may find your own ideas about God stretched or altered as you read through this section.

What beliefs have helped you to attain a better relationship with God?

LYNN ANDREWS

I remember one time when I was sitting with my teachers in Nepal, at the foot of the Himalayas and crying as I thought about the amount of pain and disease in the world. I took a spoonful of sugar and dumped it into a river that was coursing by. Of course, the sugar was gone in an instant. I said to my teacher, "Agnes, that's how I feel. All the work I've done in this lifetime is gone, like that sugar in the river." To think there were billions of people I never could reach filled me with agony. Agnes just laughed, because I was taking myself so seriously. Then she said something I'll never forget: "Your only true responsibility in life is to enlighten yourself— because that's all you can do. In the process of that enlightenment, you can touch others along the path." That philosophy has helped me in my relationship with God.

The other understanding that's helped me is to realize that God is a state of being and a quality of love and beauty rather than a person you dialogue with.   Having been raised in Catholic schools, I first looked for God the way one would seek a relationship with a person. It's a very different experience to realize that your own being is a reflection of the Great Spirit—and that by going within you can experience its bliss.

MARILYN ATTEBERRY

To quote a well-known song, "I believe for every drop of rain that falls, a flower grows." A trusting toddler, pointing to her heart, said, "Jesus lives right here, Gramma." I believe the Golden Rule. I believe I reap what I sow. I believe in the cycles of nature, the one-ness of all creation, and the trustworthy nature of the sun . . . it always rises. I believe human beings are inherently worthy and that God will never forsake us. I believe in guardian angels and a Holy Spirit. I have never witnessed a death, but I'm sure it can be as beautiful and heart-opening as birth. I know that life regenerates itself and that there are more universes than I have cells in my body and more stars in each universe than I have cells in my body. I believe there is a basic wisdom available to all human beings that can solve any problem. I DON'T believe that this wisdom belongs to any culture or religion. I believe it is God-sourced and totally reliable and available when one knows it is there. I believe peace is here NOW.

PAT BOONE

I believe it's quite possible to achieve success in any field by employing the right approach to prayer. What kind of destiny can you look forward to, can any of us look forward to, apart from His active participation in our lives? I am convinced that the "fearful" aspect of the relationship [with God] comes from lack of knowledge, the factor of the unknown, and that increased involvement and productive communication begins to wipe all the fear away.

Most of us want a lot of things, and probably most of those things are good in themselves. *But*—money and power and influence, almost every *thing* that we might want, brings with it some kind of responsibility. The greater the goals, the greater the maturity required to cope with them properly. And maturity only comes through knowledge and experience. Because God truly loves us, and because He's infinitely wiser than we are, He *can't* give us everything we ask for, right when we ask for it—any more than you can with *your* kids!

JOAN BORYSENKO

I can't say I have any *beliefs* in God that are really helpful because my beliefs have changed so much. All I can rely on is experiences I've had, or the experiences I've heard about through others. Having worked in a hospital setting with critically ill people, I've been present at a number of deathbeds. Because death is like birth, I've sometimes experienced a tremendous sense of the Divine Presence when people were dying. I see death as a gateway into the Mystery. I've heard people near death talk about their pre-death visions, or about their near-death experiences in which they see the Light. Every time I hear about being in the presence of the Light, and on those rare occasions when I have experienced the Light, I feel God's presence. For me, being around and hearing about such experiences is really important. It's also helpful to read about them. Many people reading this book will be reminded of what it is like to be in the presence of God. Because of that, they'll be able to experience it more easily, or actually experience it through reading the words in the book.

LeVar Burton

I believe that God and consciousness are interchangeable terms for the same thing. Now, here's the wild thing about being a human being: God decided to conduct an experiment. God said, "Let's create a scenario in which we will experience ourselves as consciousness through the most amount of density possible. We will immerse ourselves in an experience of physical density, and the game will be to remember that we are God—despite being in physical forms." I know that I agreed to come in and create for myself and others triggers to the knowledge that we are God. That's why I've become a filmmaker—so I could create entertainment vehicles that cause us to remember who we are.

I see acting as a way of burning karma. I've experienced many, many lifetimes through the characters that I've played. There have been karmic debts that have been resolved through the portrayal of these characters. Acting is also a very powerful way of dealing with the emotional self. It's a great gift and a tremendous trap for actors to be so facile at manipulating emotions. So the real challenge for me as an actor is to allow my facility for expressing emotion to be present in my own life. That takes an awful lot of courage.

Mantak Chia

In the Taoist way, we believe that in order to feel God, you need to feel inside of you the energy we call "chi." Since God is energy, we believe that God is also chi. We call God *Wu Chi*, which means the supreme ultimate chi. Furthermore, we believe that if you can refine and conserve your energy, you can go to the place people call "heaven." But if you scatter your life force, you remain in this world and suffer in it. In Taoism, we don't say that if you believe in some Holy person you go to heaven, and that otherwise you go to hell. Instead, by conserving and refining your own energy, you can go to heaven.

DEEPAK CHOPRA

Each of us inhabits a reality lying beyond all change. Deep inside us, unknown to the five senses, is an innermost core of being, a field of non-change that creates personality, ego, and body. This being is our essential state—it is who we really are.

ALAN COHEN

An intimate relationship with God takes time. The thought that I don't have time to create that space is just an illusion. As creative, masterful souls, there's always a way for us to hook up with our Source. In my workshops I have people make a list. They draw a line down the center of a page, and on the left side they write all the things they really love to do—things that make them feel alive, empowered and inspired. On the right side they write the activities that drain their energy and make them feel less than they were when they started. Making that list is very enlightening. You get to see the ways that you empower yourself and the ways that you debilitate yourself. When you start to become aware of that, the motivation to shift comes naturally.

People who aren't creating time and space for Spirit are either unaware that they have the power to be happy or they're afraid of love. In my workshops, I create a space that's very intimate, and I do it very gently. I make it safe for the heart to open and for people to come out. And in that space of welcome and warmth, people naturally want to be more intimate. They also become very aware of the ways that they're blocking themselves—for example, sometimes people start to get sick or angry, or they start to get depressed. All these things that are unlike love come up in a space of love, and that's really a good sign, because it means that is what's up for healing. Once people become aware of the past pains they were holding onto, they can begin to let them go. The result is that they create more space for God.

STAN DALE

I think there's either love or there's violence; there is either love or a cry for love. As it became apparent to me that when human beings are violent, they're just crying out for love, incredible amounts of compassion began to swell up in my heart. We keep trying to make God into a bearded old man when in reality He is inside all of us. God represents our own magnificence and love coming forth.

RAM DASS

What has been seen as a liability in me and my teachings—namely, that I'm an eclectic—I think I've turned into a strength because my experience of God can come through a lot of different systems. I assume that every religion has been rooted in some mystical or transcendent experience, and from that assumption, I just look at all the different systems as metaphors or doorways to God. I really enjoy the many doorways without getting confused about what's beyond each doorway.

As far as beliefs go, I'm not very attracted to beliefs because although they point you in the right direction, they don't keep you warm on a cold night. A belief allows for doubt, and I would say that what carries me home is my faith. Now if you ask me what faith is, I'd say that it's something that isn't open to question any longer. I've had so many experiences and I've met so many spiritual teachers who touched me so deeply, that what started out as "belief" finally became "this is the way it is." Of course, being inundated with all these experiences was certainly a prerequisite for developing this faith.

BRUCE DAVIS

I believe that spiritual practices need to be working with the heart, and that the main ways of opening the heart are through devotion and forgiveness. The flower of devotion initially opens the heart, and forgiveness is what keeps an open heart free from bitterness. In the Bible, Jesus says we need to forgive seven times seventy. I believe the reason he said those words is that when we forgive that much, we begin to understand how much we are forgiven and accepted by God. We begin to understand how bright and intense God's love really is.

I also believe that most people don't experience God's grace because they're so filled up with the dream of daily life. They try to integrate spirituality with being preoccupied with the daily world—and the two don't mix. You really have to create a space in your heart that's just for God. Slowly, the roots of daily life inside ourselves become less deep. When we're filled with the roots of "I want this" and "I'm busy with that", the roots of the daily dream are too deep to allow the divine roots to really grow. All the religions talk about how we are in this world but not of it; you need to create some sense of separation until you have a space inside that's just you and God.

WAYNE DYER

I think there is a divine order to the whole universe and to all our experiences. At one time I thought that this was an accidental universe, in which you just sort of show up, and then you're gone. But then I began to be aware that we're all part of an intelligent system   There's an invisible organizing intelligence that we're all part of, and we're all here for a reason. We come from nowhere to now here, and we're here for some heroic mission. When I put all that together in my mind, I realize that our purpose must have to do with the opposite of getting. We come in with nothing and we leave with nothing. The only thing you can do with your life is give it away.

I've also found it helpful to get beyond the orthodoxy of spiritual experience—instead of becoming Christian, to become Christ-like; instead of being Buddhist, to be Buddha-like. Spiritual experiences don't come through training or through having someone else push a set of rules on you; they come when the student is ready. When the student is ready, the teacher will appear. When you don't have the right degree of readiness, even if a teacher or a teaching knocks you over the head, it won't make any difference. And the way to get ready is to create a deep knowing that there's more to life than this physical form we all find ourselves in.

WARREN FARRELL

I feel as if I have a sense of what religion and God were about in the past and what they can be about now. In the past, formal religion gave us strict rules to follow, like "no sex before marriage." These rules were designed to make us want to marry, have children, and protect those children until those children were old enough to repeat the process. (Sex before marriage would have led to unprotected children; masturbation and homosexuality would have tempted people to have sexual pleasure without 18 years of responsibility.) So in the past the rules of religion had to prioritize survival over self-fulfillment, and we often prayed to God to ask for help with all the responsibilities we undertook in the process of helping a family of 10 survive. Religion established rules for mortality and called them rules for morality.

Nowadays, the type of people who read books like this one do not have to be preoccupied with survival; we are free to look inside ourselves and listen for what would help us to create harmony. This was not a luxury we had when we had to kill animals and other people that threatened our survival. Now, in a world of enormous options, we need to tune into the God inside ourselves to decide which options are best to take. This is the first time in history that we've had this luxury, so we have a new opportunity in the way we approach God.

WILLIS HARMAN

The primary belief I have—which is really less a belief than a knowing—is that there is nothing to fear, and that one can totally trust. In addition, I suspect that when I have my most profound spiritual encounters, I am still experiencing God through an intermediary; it's a higher level of myself that is, or contains, the essence of the Divine.

My knowledge of a Higher Power has been a progressive revelation, spread over the last forty years. At any point, it transcends by far anything I could have imagined a decade earlier. In my experience, any concept one may have of God will be a block to establishing the relationship so devoutly sought. The way to avoid such blocking is to have intention without expectation and trust without belief.

RICHARD HATCH

I believe that all people are artists. I believe that all people are creative but that we block ourselves from expressing our creative energy. Yet, when we give ourselves permission to express ourselves, we become co-creators with God. The reason most people don't do this is because they first have to turn around and face themselves. They have to face what they've been running away from for so long. Only by embracing and expressing their pain can people transmute these hidden parts of themselves. But by going through that process, they can begin to fulfill their divine purpose as a creative artist.

I don't think you can pay lip service to God. You can't just go to church on Sunday. God is like having a child that totally disrupts your life. When you first have a child, your life is very different because you're not used to constantly taking care of someone else. But as the child lives with you for several months, you start to adjust your life, and taking care of the child becomes a joyous part of your life. And that's the way it is with God. At first,

God disrupts your life and your patterns, but eventually it can become part of your life and way of doing things.

God has become the most intimate relationship in my life. I believe that all our relationships in life are like training wheels— preparing us to come home to our true relationship with God. When we begin to touch our true essence, we can never settle for anything less.

LOUISE HAY

As a child I was taught self-hatred and felt very lost, unloved, and abandoned. With my limited "religious" experiences I concluded that God made people wear hairshirts and threw them to the lions, so I certainly did not want to become a Christian. When I learned many years later that I was not a bad person or a "sinner," my whole outlook on life changed. I learned that I was lovable and could even love myself. It was then that I began to develop a trusting relationship with the Universe. I discovered that God was not an angry old man sitting on a cloud taking note of all my sins but rather a Universal Force and Power that had only good in store for me. All I had to do was learn to cooperate with the Laws of Life. Learning the Laws of Life, learning how they work, and using them has changed me and my life to such a wonderful degree that I hardly remember my difficult childhood.

JERRY JAMPOLSKY

As a kid, I felt that if I ate pork, God would strike me dead. My parents told me that. Like many children, I grew up thinking God was a man with a beard who could punish me. Nowadays, my concept of God has nothing to do with any kind of form. It has to do with a loving energy. Some of the most powerful spiritual people I've met don't even believe in

God. They just live their lives in a very kind way, passionate-
ly helping others. I don't think our labels or categories are
important. I think what matters is what we're doing in our
lives right now. Are we willing to be just a little more kind, a
little more tender, a little more compassionate?

I've seen that when I change the way I think about things, the
whole world around me changes. Many years ago my answering
service actually fired me. They said I complained more than anybody else, and they didn't want any part of me. I was very embar-
rassed. I decided to start thinking that "this moment on the
phone is the most important moment in my life." About a year
later, I got a call from someone representing my new answering
service, and this person said, "We've been reading the newspaper
about your work, and we're so impressed with it that we'd like to
offer you our services for free." I believe that changing the way
you look at things can actually change your life and the world.
What we need to do is see that there's no value to holding onto
anything in this world except the love we've given and received.

GURUCHARAN SINGH KHALSA

I've found it helpful to liken spiritual growth to an orchestra.
In an orchestra, each instrument has to be well-made. That's
a basic qualification. The orchestra also needs to be complete.
That means you need to accept the instruments you don't like
and let them be played. In spiritual terms, that's called bringing the shadow in. Shadow work is essential. Once you have
all the instruments playing, sometimes they're going to play in
harmony and sometimes not. In a similar way, sometimes the
various parts of our mind are working in tune with each other,
and sometimes there is a total cacophony. Yet, when everything is coordinated, when all the instruments are in harmony
with each other, music is made. In personal terms, I would call
such a state "health."

For health or harmony to be achieved, everything must be coordinated by a higher force. Some people get one part of themselves (their instrument) going very strong, yet it doesn't integrate very well with those of other people. Yet a good conductor can help bring everything together into a synergistic whole. The conductor makes no sound, yet he or she can be found in all of the instruments. He can lead the orchestra to play a classical piece of music, with wonderful eternal overtones that none of the individual instruments would ever have been able to produce by themselves. As the orchestra plays in a coordinated fashion, everyone is lifted into a state of ecstasy. In my analogy, the conductor represents the guidance of the guru. The guru's job is to coordinate individuals to play their own perfect notes in the Divine orchestra.

THE DALAI LAMA

Every major religion has similar ideas of love, the same goal of benefiting humanity through spiritual practice, and the same effect of making its followers into better human beings. All religions teach moral precepts for perfecting the functions of mind, body, and speech. All teach us not to lie or steal or take others' lives, and so on. The common goal of all moral precepts laid down by the great teachers of humanity is unselfishness. Those teachers wanted to lead their followers away from the paths of negative deeds caused by ignorance and to introduce them to paths of goodness. All religions can learn from one another; their ultimate goal is to produce better human beings who will be more tolerant, more compassionate, and less selfish.

KENNY LOGGINS

Everything I learned in my first 42 years was but preparation for my love affair with Spirit. Love is the goal, love is the path, love is the lesson, love is the joy, love is the pain, love is the teacher. Only in true love can the "demons" rise up to be healed. Only in true love can the "unlovable selves" see the folly of their illusion. Only in the clarity of true love can we see who we truly always have been and still are. And only by following, one by one, the fears that rise up to obscure the view of our beloved can we walk upon love's path. The road to love is lit by the lamps of fear.

EMMETT MILLER

I used to be a militant agnostic. To answer "yes" or "no" to the question, "Is there a God?" indicated to me the same basic error in logic. But then I began to learn that the sacred writings had been altered by political forces, and that maybe I hadn't gotten the straight scoop. At the same time, as a doctor I began to recognize that those people who had faith in some power got well more frequently than those people who didn't. It didn't even seem to make much difference what they were believing in; the more sincerely they believed, and the more humane goodness they perceived in the Being they followed, the deeper seemed to be the healing they went through. So in spite of myself, I began to believe in the power of belief. That was a big step for me.

Later, in my trips to Nepal and Bali, I encountered worship that was totally open and free. Children play on the religious monuments. In Bali, there's no word for religion or art because it's all part of what you do; it's not separate from life. the Balinese sense of integration made sense to me. Seeing a non-pompous way of worshipping definitely had an impact on me.

DAN MILLMAN

During my college years I had a profound experience or realization that God was One, had exploded to form the many, and had one Great Purpose: to grow back to Unity again, and this was Evolution. So I've always treated God not as a loving Being but as Love itself, as every speck of matter and energy in the Universe. Concurrent with that realization was the tacit sense that since God is everywhere, and in everything, any lack of God was my own limitation in feeling or communing with that Mystery. That experience and "belief" formed my foundation and introduction to the transcendental.

EDGAR MITCHELL

I believe that our deepest beliefs change not only the way we relate to the world but the physical world we live in. It's a powerful concept. Creating reality is a function that we have in the past traditionally ascribed only to deity. It used to be felt that if a person didn't like what was given, all one could do was supplicate a deity. In reality, if you modify the deepest aspect of your own belief system, you change the reality of your life.

From the metaphysical point of view, thought and reality are simply two sides of the same coin. When you modify the thought, you modify the reality. Someday soon we'll know how thought quantifies as energy, where it falls on the electromagnetic spectrum. Someday we'll have a better understanding of the relationship between a field of thought and a field of matter.

My experience of walking on the moon helped me look at the Earth from a different perspective, and it shook up my previous belief system. I had the insight that our scientific model of reality, particularly cosmology and causality, was flawed and incomplete. As it threw my old belief system into disarray, I had to start reassembling a new one. The experience in space was the mountain top experience—it was euphoric. But letting go of outmoded beliefs was like picking porcupine needles out of my skin. Each belief I pulled out had a little pain associated with it, because our tendency is to hang onto our ideas so tightly. Yet I think we all have to go through that process of letting go of limiting beliefs.

PAM OSLIE

I think we've been trained not to trust ourselves and to think we're "bad." I believe that's a fallacy and that we are part of God. To make a separation just creates fear, judgment and mistrust. If somebody were to ask me how I know when intuitive guidance comes from God and not from me, I say it's all the same; why even ask the question if we trust that we are not separate from God?

I believe we create our own reality from our beliefs about reality. What we have here is an illusion. It's a big movie we're creating. I know other religions say that you have to first learn certain lessons before you can experience higher levels. But I think we're already at those higher levels. We came down to create this movie just for the experience, but we fell asleep and forgot that we were responsible for creating the movie. We can wake up any time we want—we're just attached to the movie.

M. SCOTT PECK

We contemplatives pay attention not only to our outward experiences but also to our inner voices. Indeed, those of us who are religious believe that God actually often speaks to us through such voices: that they may be revelation. We further believe that a contemplative lifestyle dramatically increases either the frequency with which God speaks to us or else our capacity to hear Her.

It takes time—thinking time or contemplative time—to discern whether a dream is pregnant with hidden meaning or whether it is more likely a mere distraction resulting from random neuronal activity. It takes time to test all our inner messages (after we've taken the time to listen to them in the first place), to check them out against reality and reason and experience, to question their wisdom and creativity.

PETER RUSSELL

I do have one belief, and that is that beliefs stand in the way of our experience of higher consciousness or God. The Buddha said, "Don't believe anything I have said; only when it is part of your experience should you believe it." I find that beliefs sidetrack us. They trap the mind.

In the Sufi tradition there's a story about God and the devil taking a walk together. God stoops down and picks up something from the ground and shows it to the devil and says, "Look at this, it's a piece of truth. The truth is everywhere. Isn't it a concern of yours that people can find the truth so easily? " The devil replies, "It doesn't bother me at all, because with a little help from me, they soon will turn that truth into a belief." I feel there's a lot of meaning in that story.

Beliefs stem from the need of the ego. The ego likes to have things to hold onto. The ego likes to feel secure, and beliefs help it feel secure. But when I'm in touch with my preferred state of consciousness, I don't need that security. What is, IS. That is all that's important. The fact that people actually kill each other over their differing beliefs about God shows how caught up we can get in our beliefs. For me, there's nothing I'm certain of. That uncertainty makes me more receptive to new information and experiences. If I'm feeling more at peace, that is undeniable. That doesn't need belief.

BERNIE SIEGEL

First, I have to preface this by saying that what is different about me is that in 1991 I served on the Board of Directors of Heaven as an outside advisor. I therefore have a lot of inside information that many other people don't have. I feel that the universe or God is on our side. If it were not on our side, we would bleed to death or die of an infection every time something happened to us. But our wounds heal beneath the bandages. Our body loves us. This says to me that God is trying to help me; God is a resource. As life changes, I become part of this creative energy and force. We work together, so I experience that love and energy in everything I do. The riderless horse knows the way to the barn. We need to let go of the reins of our intellect.

My hope is—and this may sound crazy—that one day I will win the lottery so I can say to people, "Oh God, why me?" Because when somebody gets a life-threatening illness, people say, "Oh God, why me?" I think we have to clarify that God isn't up there deciding all those things. Catastrophes happen, difficulties happen, but God is a resource that can help us survive adversity. Out of the pain, what choice do we make? I think when you realize you're mortal, you have to make a choice: what do you want to do with your limited amount of time? Jung believed that God needs human beings to assist in the incarnation of His creation. I sometimes think it can be very hard to just feel God loving you— you need God to have skin; you need a person to love you.

In heaven, after people get in, they turn back toward the Earth and say, "Why was I so serious back there?" I think that it's really important to keep laughing at the craziness, the human comedy. I think God has a sense of humor. By the way, nowadays when I lecture, I refer to God as a woman. I think the feminine aspect is much more God-like, and we need more of it in our society.

MARSHA SINETAR

My relationship is not belief (although I have a decided set of religious convictions). Relationship with God is both my radical, direct knowledge—and yes, my faith—that the living,

Holy Spirit is not a belief but, as the book of Galatians so sweetly puts it, is Christ actually living me. This is the precise heart of my insight.

BROTHER DAVID STEINDL-RAST

My beliefs about God have changed in the process of my development. James Fowler's book, *Stages of Faith*, maps out the faith development of a person, just as Piaget mapped out the intellectual development of children. So my notions of God have changed as I've moved from stage to stage. Earlier, I had the idea of God as a parent figure, and that was very reassuring to me. As my ideas of God have developed, I've tried to not throw the baby out with the bath water. Currently, I think of God as almighty, but not in the sense that we usually conceive of almightyness. Rather, I think of God as almighty in the sense that love, compassion, and wisdom overcome everything. They overcome not by power as we conceive it normally but by the power of weakness, the power of vulnerability.

Unfortunately, all the different religions have a tendency to become institutionalized and to become an obstacle as much as they are a help. I do not believe that the religions make a person religious. They can help, but I think that everybody who belongs to a religious tradition has a responsibility to make that religion religious. It's our responsibility, not the other way around.

RON SMOTHERMAN

I have come to the conclusion that life is designed for the training of the soul. For this, a body is necessary, along with all the limitations of awareness that a body implies. I believe that the soul is created by God with the potential to itself become Godly, but that the individual soul must search on its own for the Truth that creates this Godliness. Any belief swallowed whole from the experience of others is useless and merely a distraction.

CHARLES TART

I believe that the talent and life situation I've been given can be used for good in the world. One of the reasons I've been effective with the kind of people I've been able to help is because I'm not a mystic. I have had to go on my intelligence, rely on my values, and be scientific about my spiritual search. People who are intellectuals like me, who value science and reason, will listen to me much more than they will somebody who comes in and says, "God told me to tell you this." So I think I've been blessed by not having mystical experiences. It's enabled me to share something with people for whom those experiences would be a barrier.

MOTHER TERESA

To me, God and compassion are one and the same. Compassion is the joy of sharing. It's doing small things for the love of each other—just a smile, or carrying a bucket of water, or showing some simple kindness. These are the small things that make up compassion.

Compassion means trying to share and understand the suffering of people. And I think it's very good when people suffer. To me, that's really like the kiss of Jesus. And a sign, also, that this person has come so close to Jesus, sharing his passion.

It is only pride and selfishness and coldness that keep us from having compassion. When we ultimately go home to God, we are going to be judged on what we were to each other, what we did for each other, and, especially, how much love we put in that. It's not how much we give, but how much love we put in the doing—that's compassion in action.

MARIANNE WILLIAMSON

Belief in God is not a particularly meaningful concept. Ultimately it's the experience of God that matters. A universal theology is not necessary, but a universal experience is. As *A Course In Miracles* student, I know the *Course* is not trying to get us to believe in God. It's trying to get us to believe in one another. The belief in one another *is* the experience of God.

I don't think connecting with God is a Mysterious process. In fact, I think it's important to demystify the process. Meditation connects us, prayer connects us, forgiveness connects us. It's not that we don't know what to do, it's that we resist doing the things we know work. Spiritual exercise is like physical exercise; when we do it, it works. But we come up with excuses for not doing what it takes, including, "I can't meditate right now because I'm too busy saving the planet." I think the biggest help we can give the planet is to meditate enough each day.

"I believe that God is in me, as the sun is in the colour and fragrance of a flower, the Light in my darkness, the Voice in my silence."
HELEN KELLER

7

What Does God Want

*"The measure of a person's knowledge is the
actions they take."*
ST. FRANCIS OF ASSISI

Holy books, such as the Bible or the Koran, are filled with
instructions regarding the way God wants us to behave. If all
these books agreed with each other, our task in life would be
easy. But they don't. Some holy books even contradict themselves, such as directing us in one part of the book not to kill
people, and then in another part of the book saying it's okay
to kill the enemies of God. God help us sorting through all
this information!

I asked the experts "What does God want from us?" in
order to see if there was general agreement regarding what we
are supposed to do to "please" God. The implications of the

answers to this question are immense. If we can't agree what God basically "wants" from us, then we are forever destined to move in different directions from those on other spiritual paths. Yet, if we can agree there is a basic bottom-line "job" God has given us to do, then we are all united in a common challenge. If we really all share the same goal, then we can all help each other get there.

Someone once said that life is the only game in which the object is to learn the rules. What are the "rules" for spiritual growth and for doing "God's will?" What, if anything, does God want from us? And for God's sake, why can't He make Himself more clear?! Perhaps some of the answers that follow will resonate with you. If you read something that feels "right" for you, perhaps that *feeling* is God's way of saying, "This is what I want from you."

*What, if anything, do you think
God wants from us?*

MARILYN ATTEBERRY

I think God wants us to love ourselves, love each other, laugh compassionately at life and live all aspects of the human experience within a context of trust, peace, and joy. I think God always wants us to be honest with ourselves and live from that place of vulnerable truth . . . and to be easy on ourselves when we forget. And be brave! I'm sure God means for life to be a lot of fun.

PAT BOONE

God is not only the Giver of speech—He means to be one of the prime *objects* of speech. I believe that's unquestionably the truth. And now put yourself in His place for just a moment. Or, in a simpler context, imagine yourself a parent whose child never speaks to you. You've done a great many good things for the child, you love that child enough to die for him or her, and you feel that the child is at least vaguely aware of your existence—but he or she never speaks to you at all! Wouldn't that distress you, displease you, perhaps even grieve you. Though spoken words are so vital in every other area of our lives, it's amazing to me that so many people neglect an area of interpersonal communication so important to personal and social growth as prayer.

I truly believe that, in a very real sense, God is like the Chairman of the Board who founded the company and who wants to bring His sons up through the structure he created, learning the business from the ground up, eventually reaching the place where they can take over, completely! His number one Son accomplished more in His life, achieving total manhood and lordship over all things in a very short lifetime, than anyone else in history—or all the rest of us put together! And I'm going to share with you the secret of His success: *He only and always did His Father's will.* You can call it religion—I call it practicality. It works!

JOAN BORYSENKO

The purpose of life seems to be about love. From listening to people's near-death experiences, I know that when we look back on the experiences in our life, we'll look at how well we were able to love the people we encountered in our life. We'll see how well we encouraged other people. So I would say the divine will is to encourage the unique potential in each of us to come out—to express itself. And the way to do that is through love.

DEEPAK CHOPRA

The transformation from separation to unity, from conflict to peace, is the goal of all spiritual traditions.

ALAN COHEN

I don't think God wants anything. I think God is beyond a state of want. Want implies lack, and Spirit is totally devoid of lack. It's always in a state of Grace and wholeness. The notion of God wanting something from us is really just a projection of our wanting something from God. But there is a level at which we could play the game, and I would say that if God wants anything, it's just for us to love ourselves and to see ourselves as God sees us. It's really our need, not God's, to do that.

STAN DALE

God wants us to get in touch with our perfection, magnificence, and love. The reason that we treat each other and the planet so poorly is that we treat ourselves so poorly. There's never been another human being on this planet like you. Yet most of us don't think we're worth anything: we think we're too old or too young or too fat or too thin, or whatever. I ask people to tell me anything that makes them less than magnificent. Usually they'll tell me just little piddly stuff. God wants us to recognize our inherent beautiful innocence. Look at the eyes of a child who hasn't yet been programmed that he or she is not okay. It's eyes and face are like a wide open "Wow!" That's what God wants from us.

RAM DASS

If you look at the vast cycles of time, from the evolution of emptiness into form, and then form into consciousness, and finally consciousness awakening to its predicament, I could say that what God wants of itself is to awaken to the point where there is only God within itself. It's like a hide-and-seek game in which God goes to sleep and then slowly awakens back into itself. Ultimately, God has a fully conscious mirroring of itself as the separate entity fully awakens to the point where it experiences no more separateness. It's a long process of coming into dualism and then going back out of dualism. Rather than saying what "God wants," which is a funny term, I would say that God IS this whole process.

WAYNE DYER

I think God "wants" us to exercise our free will to keep our lives on purpose and to serve others. That's when I'm happiest. My mantra before I speak or before I write is always "How can I serve?" I just ask that question over and over again. And when I do that for 45 minutes before I speak to an audience, I go out there and it's bliss. I don't miss a beat. I find myself flawlessly quoting poetry that I didn't even know I knew! Everything works perfectly when I move away from thinking things like, "How much am I going to make?" or "Are they going to like me?"

The glue that holds every cell in our bodies together, and the glue that holds the universe together, is love. A cell inside a body that is cancerous is one that will gobble up the cell adjacent to it because it has no identification with the whole, whereas a cell that is healthy will stay at peace with the cell adjacent to it. I think that each one of us is like a single cell in a body called humanity, and we have dis-ease when we want to fight with the people next to us. By finding ease within ourselves and serving our connection to the whole, we can all live in harmony.

WARREN FARRELL

I think the part of ourselves that is God wants us to contribute to harmony and to empowering others as often as possible. What goes around comes around. When you help and support others, others then want to give back to you. By attending to the conscious part of ourselves, we contribute to the peace of others as well as ourselves.

RICHARD HATCH

I think God wants us to express ourselves fully. When we express ourselves without judgment, we are doing what God created us to do; we are in alignment with God's energy. At our core we are divine artists, and God expresses himself through us. God is not separate from humans. What God wants is what we all want, to express in any way our heart desires this magnificent life-force within each one of us. If we feel like screaming, we are supposed to scream. If we feel like dancing in that moment, God would want us to dance. God wants us to celebrate, to express his energy without judgment or fear and with unconditional love.

WILLIS HARMAN

My direct experience is that my higher Self, the divine "I," does in fact want me to consciously identify with that Self and, eventually, with the Whole. My own fears, rooted in my concept of separateness, prevent this from being the case fully. If I were to say that my Self or Christ-consciousness, wants anything, it is that I should realize that supreme identity.

LOUISE HAY

I believe God wants us to be joyful and to share in the great abundance that is available to each and every one of us. We are here to laugh, have fun, and to love ourselves, each other, and every other living creature. We are here to take care of Mother Earth and to treat her with great reverence. We are here to play. The Universe rejoices when we take advantage of all the good it has to offer.

JERRY JAMPOLSKY

We're here to co-create and be messengers of love. We're here to heal the illusion of separation that is here on Planet Earth. We're here to forgive. I sometimes ask people, "If you were going to die tomorrow and someone was going to write one sentence about you, what would you want it to say?" I've asked this question to a lot of people, and they never mention their bank account or what kind of car they drive. They usually say something like, "He did his best job to be kind and loving to others." When you look at your own life and compare it to what you would want people to say about you, oftentimes there is a discrepancy. Many of us have gotten off track. I think God wants us to live our lives on purpose.

THE DALAI LAMA

I feel that my mission is, wherever I am, to express my feeling about the importance of kindness, compassion, and the true sense of brotherhood. I practice these things. It gives me more happiness, more success. If I practiced anger or jealousy or bitterness, no doubt my smile would disappear.

KENNY LOGGINS

We are the fallen angels sent here to find love through fear. Our task is to learn to trust.

EMMETT MILLER

I think that what God wants of us is the discovery of oneness, releasing our illusion of separateness.   There's an old story about God granting to a man who had lived a very saintly life his wish to visit both heaven and hell. When he visited hell, everywhere he looked he saw tables and tables piled high with delicious food. Sitting around these tables were very, very thin people, each with a six-foot-long spoon in their hand. Each was spending all of eternity trying to get the spoon into his or her mouth but couldn't because the handle was too long. Then God took the saintly man to heaven, and in heaven the scene looked the same: Delicious food and people who had spoons with six-foot-long handles. But in heaven, everyone looked well-fed. The difference was, that in heaven, people had learned to feed each other.

To discover that oneness—that we give to ourselves when we give to another—is what you could say God wants. There's a place in you and a place in me where, when we're in that part of ourselves, there is only one of us.

DAN MILLMAN

To ask what "God wants" seems to imply that God is an other, who has attachments and desires. I don't feel God works that way. To me, God is the inherent, profound, all-powerful Force and Substance of everything. God feels like the Creator and the Creation.

EDGAR MITCHELL

This question goes directly to the heart of the purpose of the universe. Science has said there is no purpose; religion has fundamentally said God's purpose is enigmatic. I can only hypothesize that the deepest purpose of the universe is to organize itself; to continue to create a more idyllic permanent physical experience. For us that means to organize our lives in more fruitful, productive, and harmonious ways. To recognize that we're all of the same body, that the God within is collectively the God without, that we're all a part of the same consciousness. We're all creating our reality together. It's the sum total of all of us creating reality that makes reality. So our purpose is to create an ever-evolving learning system with greater levels of complexity and harmony. That seems to be at the heart of our purpose.

PAM OSLIE

God wants us to just experience love and not to limit our experiences—not to judge ourselves. I don't think God needs anything from us, but He wants us to experience and express ourselves in lots of different ways and forms. Sometimes it'll be fun and sometimes it'll be painful. I think one of the reasons we (God and us) made physical reality is so we could experience the whole range of emotions. God notices when we begin believing we are stuck in something and says, "Of course you can get out of it: simply wake up." So I guess you could say God wants us to wake up and, instead of living in pain, be conscious creators again.

M. SCOTT PECK

I believe that God calls each and every human being to civility. This means we are all under the obligation to become more conscious, to grow in spiritual competence, and to strive to be ethical in our behavior.

BERNIE SIEGEL

I think we're here to love the world. God can get lonely, so He put up mirrors to reflect His Light and love back. People are the reflectors of this original love. As a physician, I once tried to cure everything, so I was burning out. I was miserable, and my patients told me that I needed to learn how to live. I no longer feel that I have to get everybody on their feet. If I can help them live their lives, then healing has taken place. And the main thing we have to offer each other is listening to each other.

I'm now writing a book that describes life as a labor pain. We are here to give birth to ourselves, so the pain is a part of the process. I think individuals who are confronting afflictions and adversity are really doing God's work. I know a young man who said, "If God wanted me to be a basketball player, He would have made me seven feet tall, but He gave me cancer so I'd write a book and help other people."

MARSHA SINETAR

I think God wants pure, unbroken, devoted relationship. Worshipful, wholly self-renunciated, grateful union. God is our Parent, Friend, Healer, Lover, and Provider and a jealous one at that: *"Thou shalt have no other gods before me."* This line states expressly that God wants our *total, undiluted fidelity*, our complete unadulterated attention, which is love. As Thomas Merton taught again and again, to want, (or involve ourselves with) anything besides this one great Good, to desire to add knowledge of anything else to experience, is to turn away from life and from Reality itself. This is my most basic, entry-level experience of what, as you put it, "God wants from us."

BROTHER DAVID STEINDL-RAST

Philosophically, the notion of God is completeness, so God couldn't possibly want anything from us. But mystically, in the religious experience one encounters God like a lover who wants no less than your whole self. God wants your full aliveness. In the second century, a famous Christian mystic said, "The glory of God is the human being who is fully alive."

RON SMOTHERMAN

I consider life to be a training assignment. The task of the training is to live fully by striving to master the ability to be loved and the ability to be loving. Counting the most in life, I believe, are the small things we do in intimate relationships, where one has the opportunity to be kind, to be understanding, and to contribute. These are the places where true opportunity exists.

CHARLES TART

I think what's wanted by God is our authenticity. I don't want to say there's some kind of specific rule, because too many people like me have a superego that's too hard on them already. Yet I'm very impressed by the two answers regarding the purpose of life given by people who have had near-death experiences. From their mystical rendezvous with death, the most common answer they give is that the purpose of life is to learn how to love. The second most common answer they give is that the purpose of life is to contribute to human knowledge. Both of those answers resonate deeply in my heart.

MOTHER TERESA
All God really wants is for us to love Him. The way we can show our love for Him is to serve others.

MARIANNE WILLIAMSON
He wants us to love one another, that we might be set free from our pain.

"Work out your salvation with diligence."
BUDDHA, IN HIS LAST COMMAND TO HIS DISCIPLES

8

Finding God In Daily Life

*"Though I walk through the valley of the
shadow of death, I will not fear, thou art
with me."*
KING DAVID

It could be said that our awareness of God goes through various stages. At some point in our lives, we may believe in God but have no actual experience of God's presence. Later, we may become aware of God's presence in certain situations, such as during meditation, prayer, making love, or a church service. In Chapter Three, the experts explored the ways people deepen their experience of God. But how do we "tune into" God while driving a car or doing the dishes?

The average American spends approximately eleven years of life watching TV, nine years of life at work, three years of life in the bathroom, and less than a year in any kind of formal worship of God. Less than a year is little time to develop a truly intimate relationship. The ability to experience God while doing the business of life is no doubt an important skill. Unfortunately, most religious teachings have very little to say about how to "tune into" God during daily life. Many holy books and spiritual teachings stress the importance of such general behavior as right livelihood, loving your neighbor, and performing moral acts. While following such doctrines seems like a good idea, it does not necessarily lead to an *experience* of God in day-to-day life.

You'll notice a wide range of answers to this question. If a response touches you in some way, try it in *your* daily life. Perhaps it will bring new beauty and wonder to what used to be "mundane" tasks.

How do you remember and/or tune into the sacred during your everyday life?

MARILYN ATTEBERRY
Having people in my life whom I love is the quickest and most effective way of remembering God in my life. Rolling over in bed in the morning and seeing my husband Warren is another. Going to my office to work to create empowering experiences for other people works. And seeing my roommate Jacquie smiling as she deals with a dad who has Alzheimer's disease does the trick, too. I have a host of angels suspended from my bedroom ceiling (glass, plastic, cloth, wood), and each morning as I open my eyes, and each night before I close them, they remind me of God. Singing works, too, especially with my granddaughter.

PAT BOONE

I often just thank God spontaneously when I notice Him doing something for me or someone else. When I'm eating in a crowded restaurant, for example, I'll remember God regularly gives me and my family enough to eat, so, rather than offering a long-winded prayer that might attract undue attention, I'll just raise my eyes to heaven and say, "Thanks, Lord!"

JOAN BORYSENKO

I find God in my daily life through the practice of gratitude. My major spiritual practice is to look around me with a sense of gratitude. When I do that I feel more and more connected to everything. I feel a sense of expansiveness and an openness of the heart. To help me tune into the feeling of gratitude, it helps me to be aware of where my mind is throughout the day. If my mind is busy ruminating or judging, I take a couple of deep breaths and let go of the fear and enter into the love. Sometimes I'll think, "Let me see and fully appreciate one thing of beauty." By making that *choice*, I feel reconnected.

LEVAR BURTON

For me, the breath is a great trigger for the place God lives. I take a breath with the thought that I am breathing to become present in this moment. Whenever I feel tense in my body, it's a sign that an opening for fear has been created. Whenever I feel anxious, it's a sign to me that something is out of alignment. I then take the opportunity to take a conscious breath, to breathe in God.

I also remember God when I meet myself as God in another human being; for instance, when Stephanie, my wife, does something that brings up emotion in me, I think that God as Stephanie is reminding God as LeVar where I need to grow.

After many years of training myself, I find that strong emotions are now a trigger for me to look at something. I think that all emotions are triggers for us to grow in our level of consciousness.

MANTAK CHIA

You can tune into the Tao by always being aware of your own energy. While doing any activity you can feel the energy or chi flowing through various parts of your body. This chi is the same energy as the Wu Chi, the ultimate energy known as God. Also, by being happy in what you're doing, you're connecting with the Life Force. When people feel sadness or doubt, they lose energy and are unable to feel the Tao.

ALAN COHEN

To find God in daily life I look for beauty. I make a conscious choice not to miss this moment. If there is something that I "have to do," I'll recognize that I can choose a slight shift in perspective and really enjoy doing it. *A Course in Miracles* asks the question, "Would you rather be right or happy?" Another lesson in the *Course* reminds us, "I could see peace instead of this." So I might ask myself, "How would I be doing this if I were doing it peacefully? How else would I be thinking about this?" Usually if I ask, the shift comes. I find an angle that makes whatever I'm doing lighter. It's only when I'm really intent on being stuck that I stay stuck.

RAM DASS

I use several things. If, for example, I'm waiting in a supermarket line, I'll do an exercise in which I'll practice seeing behind the veils of who people think they are. Since I know people are so much more than they think they are, I look for that. Although I see the externals, I keep training myself to look more deeply. You could say that I'm looking for their souls. I use my intuitive mind to sense that other part of their being. You have to be resting in that place in yourself to see it in someone else.

I also use my mala beads. I'm constantly holding my beads and reciting, "Ram, Ram, Ram," with each bead that passes through my fingers. So if I'm in a social situation or somewhere in traffic, and I'm caught in whatever is going on, I'll feel a bead against my fingers and it'll remind me to begin repeating the name of God (Ram). The minute that happens, I start to see the situation I've been stuck in as just another situation.

It used to be that I generally felt a heavy sense of separation. Occasionally, through meditation, drugs, or whatever, I would get to experience a sense of lightness and being in tune with it all. But over the years, my identity has shifted so that I no longer experience that heavy, separate thing as "me." It's more as if I am God, who is temporarily playing at "me-ness." And when it starts to get too thick in "me, " I start to feel a heaviness that triggers me to awaken. I immediately begin my practice, such as saying my mantra, singing praises to Hanuman, or whatever I've got going. I don't even stop to ask "What do I feel thick about?"

Bruce Davis

To find God in daily life I use a mantra (a word or phrase with a spiritual sound and/or meaning). Over the years I've used many different mantras. The one I enjoy now is, "Lord Jesus Christ, have mercy on me." After awhile, the mantras sort of begin singing automatically, without my having to think them. There are Hindu and Buddhist mantras that are beautiful, too. Whatever I'm doing, the mantras help keep the song inside my heart going.

When using mantras, you have to use your heart. You have to start out with a mantra that touches you—that has some heart in it. Then, with each breath you inhale, you put your whole heart into it. And when you exhale, you imagine exhaling with your heart. So for me, "Lord Jesus Christ" is said internally while inhaling; "have mercy on me" is said while exhaling.

WAYNE DYER

I practice awe. I mean I'm in awe of the dishes, I'm in awe of my liver, I'm in awe when I play tennis, I'm in awe of it all. I'm just awestruck with the magnificence and the miraculousness and the bliss that is in this world.

WARREN FARRELL

During many moments in the day I feel deeply appreciative. That makes me feel God's blessings. If I'm making a microwave dinner for example, I'll think to myself about the people who planted the seeds that created the wheat. Then I'll think about the migrant workers who picked the fruit and vegetables. I'll even think about the truckers who brought the food to the market and the people checking it out at the counter. All those things are occurring so that I can have this dinner for about five minutes of my labor. That whole understanding takes about three seconds, and yet it creates in me an incredibly warm feeling of appreciation for humanity and how fortunate I am.

I also tune into this appreciation when I take the garbage out or look at someone like the garbage man or a construction worker. I've begun to really look at these people and see them as opposed to just seeing the roles they play. I recognize that their occupations can be dangerous and that such people risk their lives to construct our buildings or take away our garbage. It's a very different feeling when I take time to appreciate such people. They sparkle in my everyday life as the stars do in the nighttime sky: they make me feel both finite and yet interconnected to a grander whole.

WILLIS HARMAN

I remember to attend to my Identity—to feel the awe, the love, the oneness of God in my daily life by sensing that what IS is totally wonderful—that nothing needs to be changed. When I forget this, I notice "negative feedback": things not going well, absence of "miracles" and "marvelous coincidences," life showing signs of falling apart. Some years ago I would not catch this early enough, and would have to live through some extended period of depression, confusion, or pain. Now I typically find that the response is prompt, and I am quickly back in touch with my Self.

LOUISE HAY

I find God in my daily life by remembering as often as I can that I am a child of the Universe and that this is my playground. I am here not to judge others but to rejoice with them in the joys of living. I talk to God a lot, not with piety but as a good friend, for I know and believe that the Universe is my friend and I am always safe.

JERRY JAMPOLSKY

One of the things I do to find God in everyday life is to use little Post-It notes to remind me about God. I put them in my bathroom or in my car. They remind me how I want to feel or look at things. If something is going wrong during the day, they remind me to stop what I'm doing and start the day over again.

I try to see people as my teachers. When someone calls me on the phone for help, I try to learn from the person. In driving, I used to see the other drivers as my enemies. Now I try to see them as tremendous teachers of patience. I let go of my goals around the outcome I want and focus instead on the process of what's happening right now.

A couple of years ago I was in Poland, and my taxi driver wanted to make my receipt higher than it should have been in order to help me with my taxes. I finally said to him, "Imagine for a minute that I'm Jesus Christ, and you're having a conversation with Jesus in the back seat. Would you act differently toward me?" The taxi driver said, "Ah, I understand." He then wanted to give me money!

I sometimes do the same thing for myself. I ask, "How would Jesus respond?" I don't try to intellectualize it, I try to internalize it. Then I listen and act accordingly. It's not an intellectual process, it's a felt experience.

EMMETT MILLER

One thing I do in order to experience God in daily life is to sing. Music follows me everywhere I go. I also try to see God in each person I'm with. My belief is that we start off as pure and whole crystal reflections of the universe of God, but because of the dysfunctional environments we're brought up in, that diamond goes underground.

Having dealt with a lot of people, I've now demonstrated to my satisfaction that the divine can be found within any person. I sometimes find it in my first visit with a person, and it sometimes takes a year before I can say, "Ah, there it is. . . ." So when I see someone walking down the street, even though I haven't seen that person's heart, I've seen enough hearts to know that the diamond is in there. So I try to treat that person as if I knew that he or she were God. It's a challenge for me to have faith so alive that when I look I can see that.

DAN MILLMAN

I remember and "tune into" God by allowing my attention and feeling to rise beyond the concerns of my separate self (or mind, or ego) and look to the bigger (or transcendental) picture. It's almost like stepping out of my conscious self and seeing life from a transpersonal view of the higher self. I don't do this as a technique, or to get anywhere else (because I'm unhappy or bored), but just to remember that reality exists on different levels and not get locked entirely into the view that the separate self and its life is the only reality.

The idea that we were created in "God's image" interests me, because hidden within that statement is that we reflect God. It seems equally true that we created God in our image and that each of us tends to see God from our own state of consciousness and awareness. A person who is judgmental or vengeful, for example, may see God as judgmental; a loving person may experience God as Love.

PAM OSLIE

God is like my best friend, especially with the work I do as a professional psychic. Whenever I tune into somebody, the first thing I do is ask God to help me. Or if I'm cleaning house, I'll talk to God. I'll talk about things I want, or ask God a question and say, "Is this okay?" I'll dialogue about what's happened today or how God feels about something. If I'm feeling down, Jesus will come in and say, "Hey, how's it going?" and I'll say, "I'm feeling blocked. Can you help me with this thing?"

M. SCOTT PECK

For me Jesus has been a useful tool whenever I have had a significant dilemma and am trying to figure out my calling. At such times I simply ask, "Hey Jesus, what would you do if you were in my shoes now? How would you behave?" It is surprising how clear the answer usually is. And often how startling.

PETER RUSSELL

Whenever I'm caught up with needless thoughts, I ask myself two questions. If I'm wanting something to happen, and it's not turning out the way I want, for example, I ask, "If I get what I think I'm wanting, will it really make me feel peaceful and happy?" The answer is usually "No." Then the second question is, "Even if I don't get it, can I still be at peace?" The answer is usually "Yes." This dialogue is a way of disconnecting from the pull of the concerns that come up in my daily life.

Another thing I do is to use the *Course in Miracles*. I find that just reading a lesson each morning and then practicing the lesson during the day is most helpful. There's a different exercise for each day of the year, so you're not always doing the same thing. Each lesson points in the same direction, but you get to do it from 365 different perspectives. It's a very useful way to make the ordinary events of life become part of one's spiritual practice.

BERNIE SIEGEL

To find God in my daily life, I let the inner spirit guide me through my activities. It's helpful to not have a schedule and to let go of judgment and self-importance. Sometimes I have to stop and breathe. So if I'm caught in a traffic jam or waiting for someone to answer the phone, I just take a deep breath and let go. Then I feel connected again.

BROTHER DAVID STEINDL-RAST

I personally practice the Jesus prayer. The long form of it is "Lord Jesus Christ, Son of God, have mercy on me, a sinner." But many people use a much shorter form, such as "Lord Jesus, mercy." Mercy can stand for "Oh what mercy you are showing me," but in times of trouble it can be a cry for help. It does double duty. I repeat the Jesus prayer like a mantra. It helps me focus every moment, again and again, on the encounter with God.

CHARLES TART

I try to keep a portion of my attention on the sensations in my body as a way of grounding myself in the present. I usually forget to do it, but when I remember, it works to some extent. Sometimes I deliberately perform ordinary tasks in a different way, such as using a different pattern to brush my teeth. Such things help me avoid falling into habits in which my mind will just sort of space out and wander.

MOTHER TERESA

You may ask how the contemplative life fits together with compassion in action. It fits together by bringing union with God. Jesus said, "Whatever you do to the last of my brethren, you are doing it to me." If you do everything for Him, you are acting as a contemplative in the heart of the world.

MARIANNE WILLIAMSON

All life is everyday life. We're always thinking about things and people, whether we're in line for gasoline or in line to meet the President. The challenge is always to surrender our own will, to ask God to use us in service of healing the world, and to think with love towards all life. The universe is always listening.

*"The time of business does not differ
from the time of prayer; and in the noise and
clutter of my kitchen, I possess God in as
great tranquillity as if I were upon my knees
at the Blessed Sacrament."*
BROTHER LAWRENCE

9

In Search of the Miraculous

*"Miracles are natural. When they do not
occur something has gone wrong."*
A COURSE IN MIRACLES

What is a miracle? A definition I've found useful is the following: a miracle is anything that helps awaken us to the realization that there's more going on in this world than meets the
eye. In this sense, anything can be seen as a miracle. In an
open state of mind, a flower or a sunset can be experienced as
a miracle. Unfortunately, to awaken us to the fact that we live
in a miraculous universe, we normally need to experience
things out of the ordinary.

Western scientific thought has managed to give scientific
explanations of many events we used to consider miracles. At
one time, for example, the conception of a baby was consid-

ered a miraculous gift from the gods. Nowadays, we think of it as a clearly defined process that involves an egg, a sperm, chromosomes, and cell division. As our scientific explanations have increased, the number of events we consider miracles has decreased. Although an event *can* be described in scientific terms, it does not necessarily mean that such an explanation is valuable or accurate. A Van Gogh painting *can* be described as having a certain weight, size, and molecular structure, but such an analysis misses the entire essence of the painting.

I spent seven years with a spiritual teacher who could perform miracles. One of the things he could do was send out of his left eye an "energy beam" that would dramatically alter a person's state of consciousness for a day or two. When he would do this to me, I always felt very lucky to partake in this miracle. I would feel great bliss and love, far beyond any meditation or other special experience I ever had. Yet, one person to whom the teacher did this to thought he had been drugged, and he therefore resisted and resented the experience. He missed the "miracle" because he had his own (erroneous) explanation for the cause. From this experience I realized that even the most amazing miracles require a receptive and open mind to perceive.

The stories that follow are overflowing with God's grace, humor, and love. Reading about the miracles other people have experienced can help us be more open and inspired by the mysterious and magical world in which we live.

Have you experienced any miracles? If so,
please describe one and tell how it has affected
your faith in God.

Lynn Andrews

I once wrote about an ally I met known as the Old Crooked
One. I met her one day when I was sitting on my patio with a
cup of tea. I looked up at my lemon tree, and there she was,
perched in the tree! She had twigs in her hair, and she was
laughing. We had an incredible conversation together. We
talked about the way I get transfixed by the light that bounces
off the leaves of bamboo. We also talked about menopause. It
was a conversation held just the way you and I are sitting here
talking. For a moment I looked up at a hawk that was circling
above us, and when I turned back to the tree, she was gone.

I don't know why it's so difficult for people to accept that
there are other dimensions in reality that we can tune in and
out of at will. In describing what's going on in such situations, I
often share the story of the time I brought a radio to some
Aboriginal friends of mine in Australia. This small group had not
been touched by civilization at all. I figured they would get a
good laugh from experiencing a radio for the first time. I told
them, "this radio is like the instrument we call our bodies. It's like
an antenna that puts you in touch with other worlds." When I
turned the radio on, Beethoven's Fifth symphony seemingly
appeared out of nowhere! To them, it was a fantastic experience.
We laughed for a long time. They were fascinated by it. Later,
they asked me to take the radio back because they didn't want to
get addicted to it. They thought it would take them away from
some of the sacredness of their ceremonies. I understood.

We can all contact tremendous power and energy through
the instrument of our physical bodies We use only a tiny portion of our brains; shamanism, as I've learned it from the

Sisterhood, helps you to understand how to use what you've been given. Being able to see the Old Crooked One simply requires being in the specific state of being in which she exists. When I moved out of that state of being, she disappeared. It's possible to become stronger and stronger at entering such dimensions. It's like going to a gym to exercise your body so it'll work better. If you exercise the right part of your brain, you can learn to walk the dimensions of the universe.

MARILYN ATTEBERRY

My life itself is a miraculous occurrence in my relationship with God. My mother gave me to God the first time she held me in her arms. I have myself delivered two healthy, bright children, and they have given me three healthy, bright grand-children. I met Brandon St. John and thanks to that meeting, am in a grace-full profession that totally supports my continu-al connection with God. I have a son and a stepson who cured diseases diagnosed terminal. I married a really good man. I have had visions of angels (I'll take more, thank you), experi-enced a trip in a space ship, and had amazing amounts of ener-gy vibrating my body with undulations of bliss. And it was a drug-free high.

PAT BOONE

A couple of years ago, I had a very emotional encounter with former Black Panther leader Eldridge Cleaver, soon after his "born again" experience. After some pleasantries and some awkward attempts at getting acquainted, we all sat down around the table and joined hands to pray before we ate. Just as we were about to bow our heads, Eldridge volunteered a statement, sort of a "confession," which began a very mean-ingful prayer experience for us all.

"I can remember some of my buddies in L.A. coming

around and looking at this house and others in Beverly Hills. We were sizing it up, planning to break into this place, y'know? Of course that never happened, but here we are in this same house—getting ready to pray together. "

Deeply moved, I looked over at him and said, "Since it's true confession time, I'll tell you it's blowing my mind too—because I nearly took Debby out of school when a teacher assigned her *Soul on Ice* to read. I had read it, and even though I admired your intelligence and sympathized with some of the things you were trying to say, I didn't think this was a book for any fifteen-year-old girl, with the language and explicit sexual dreams you talked about."

Still joining hands, we bowed, and Eldridge Cleaver led us to the throne of God in prayer. And after dinner we all wound up on our knees in our den, praying and weeping together and praising God with the kind of joy I've rarely experienced before. Though a transformed personality is always a miracle, we had that special sense that Eldridge's experience was particularly dramatic and awesome—a sovereign act of an all-powerful, all-loving God.

In *A Miracle a Day Keeps the Devil Away*, I've written about thirty-one miracles that have happened to me and members of my family. Some of these are very dramatic medical miracles, a couple of them instantaneous. And so my family and I have seen multitudes of miracles, when we've joined in prayer for others. Cancers have disappeared, broken limbs have been healed instantly, hearing and eyesight have been restored, asthma and other chronic ailments have vanished, practically everything but resurrection from the dead. And a couple of our close friends have even witnessed that!

JOAN BORYSENKO

I've experienced many "miracles," but I don't know if they're highly unusual. As I go around the country I realize that a great many people have had experiences that we've been acculturated to believe are highly unusual. In fact, a Gallop poll indicated that roughly a third of Americans have had some kind of transcendent experience that lifted them out of themselves.

One of the most powerful experiences I've had was being present at my mother's death. My twenty-year-old son and I were sitting in her hospital room. I began meditating and soon had what could be called a vision. In the vision I was both a mother and a baby. I was in the process of being born, *and* I was giving birth. Along with the sense of fear that goes along with birth, there was a tremendous sense of the sacred. From my perspective as the baby, as I was born I saw a beautiful light—like the Light you hear people talk about who have near-death experiences. At that moment my entire relationship with my mother became crystal clear. I was flooded with such love and such gratitude for this relationship, even though it had in many ways been a tormented one. Suddenly I saw the wholeness of it and realized that it had been totally perfect. I had the incredible sense that my mother had given birth to my soul into this world and I was giving birth to her soul into the next world. With this overwhelming sense of love, I opened my eyes, and the whole hospital room was filled with Light. My son looked at me and said, "Can you see the Light? The room is filled with Light!" He started to weep. My son went on to say that Grandma had opened the door to eternity to give us a glimpse. He looked at me and said, "I'll never be afraid of death again, because I know now that we're immortal."

LeVar Burton

A friend of mine named Velvalee carries around a painting she did called "The Souls of Humanity." Some years ago she was directed by a voice in her head to sell everything she owned and move to Alaska. The voice was so strong that she could not deny it. While she was in Alaska she was further directed to begin work on the painting that eventually became "The Souls of Humanity." The painting is a representation of the Blessed Mother, and in her arms she holds a bouquet of roses. Cascading upward from this bouquet of roses are lights and stars representing the souls of humanity.

In the painting is a depiction of rose quartz in the shape of a heart at the breast of the Blessed Mother. Once the painting was complete, Velvalee was directed to touch the painting where the rose quartz is painted, and when she did this, she had a very profound experience. She was further directed to take this painting around the world to allow others to touch it so that they might also have a similar experience. Having grown up in the Catholic tradition, I liken this to Lourdes, or to other manifestations of the energy of the Blessed Mother. When I touched the painting for the first time three years ago at the Whole Life Expo, I had a phenomenal experience. In fact, every time subsequent to that I have felt a remarkable exchange of energy between this seemingly inanimate object and myself. My experiences with this painting have definitely affected my faith in a higher power.

MANTAK CHIA

Every time I meditate, I gather together my life force energy to develop a non-physical body that is immortal. I have no fear of death because I know how to gather all my energy and follow the clear light that comes when we die. When I meditate, I use the energy I receive to create this "second body." My physical body is not going to last forever, but whatever I can transform now in my physical body, I will have forever. That's what Jesus did. After he died, he transformed over a period of three days into a non-physical body. In the Taoist tradition are many thousands of immortals who left their physical body but have never really died because, while still alive, they created an immortal body.

ALAN COHEN

I'll tell you about one that's not especially dramatic, but it has a point. One day I was going to meet musician Charlie Thweatt. We were both going to fly into Los Angeles from different cities. In order for me to meet him when his plane was coming in, I needed to leave where I was at 5:00 A.M. When I tried that idea on for size, I couldn't see myself doing it. So I told Charlie, "The next time I can come in is 2:30 P.M., and I hate to ask you to wait four hours for me, but that's what my guidance says." He said, "Well, I'd rather not wait, but I'm willing to, if it's your guidance." I felt kind of guilty for asking him to wait, and I thought I was just being selfish. But every time I asked my inner self, it said "No, trust your intuition. Just go with it. Don't let guilt move you from your center."

I took the later plane and when I arrived at 2:30, Charlie wasn't there. After I made some calls I found out his connecting flight had been caught in a snowstorm in Denver, and he was delayed by five hours. He ended up coming in at 3:00. To me it was a really poignant lesson. When we listen to our intuition and trust the inner voice, rather than the voice of guilt and fear, everything is taken care of. That voice actually knows more than the reasoning mind.

STAN DALE

Just when the Berlin Wall collapsed, I went to Warsaw as a sort of citizen diplomat. I went into a convalescent home and visited an elderly woman who had not moved from her bed in eight years. Eight years earlier she had thrown herself under a train to commit suicide because her husband had died. I don't know why I did it, but I just kneeled at her bed and started stroking and kissing the stumps of her legs. I just kissed her and kept on loving her. After about ten or fifteen minutes she called for a wheelchair to get out of bed. The staff at the hospital couldn't believe it. They were all in tears, and so was I.

I'm still in tears when I talk to you about it. That was a miracle of God, a miracle of love, and that's what any human being on this planet can do just by being in love.

RAM DASS

Probably the most profound miracle I've experienced is the one through which I met my guru, but that's already been written about a lot. I've also been with Satya Sai Baba when he's manifested things for me, and Muktananda has let me fly. Nowadays, I'd say I experience a miracle every time I open up into the miraculous, but it's not anything so special any more. For example, I'll go see somebody with AIDS who is suffering in every possible way, and at first I'll get caught up in all their suffering; but very slowly I'll feel that heaviness or thickness within me, and I'll keep letting it go. As I let it go, *the sufferer* can let it go, and we both enter into a place of bliss and rapturous presence. We both see the whole nature of suffering and pain and death, but we both leave the situation feeling that we've touched grace. That is a miracle to me, and I think most people miss the fun of experiencing that.

When "miracles" occur, they just help to topple whatever residual faith I have in the nature of psycho-physical reality as being absolutely real. They show me once again that just behind the visible world is a whole other world in which it all works differently. They bring me to the edge of the mystery. To me, the whole art form of spiritual work is staying at the edge of the mystery all of the time. It's like surfing. You want to ride the wave. That's the perfect image. I wish I could do it more.

BRUCE DAVIS

I've experienced many miracles. I think the most intense occurred when I took a group to Assisi. On the way we stopped in Glastonbury, England, where the first temple to Mary was built. This chapel to Mary is in ruins, and there were several of us on our knees crying. We were asking her to teach us how to love her, and she appeared to us physically! The experience changed me totally. She was beautiful; she just appeared, waving her hands to us. Three other people had a vision of her, I saw her physically, but it was more real than any physical experience I've ever had.

I think spiritual experiences like that seem much more real than ordinary emotional experiences. I don't know how to explain it, but the memories of these events hit me as if they happened yesterday. I think we're given these kinds of experiences to remind us that the soul is totally real, the only thing that is real.

WAYNE DYER

A miracle happened when we were driving towards Panama City, Florida, on our vacation. My daughter was asleep in the back seat of the car with my niece. My wife was driving on a little two-lane highway, and I was deeply asleep. Suddenly, I awoke out of my deep sleep and saw a car was coming directly at the car traveling in front of us. Since my wife is much shorter than I am, she couldn't see beyond the car in front of us, so I quickly grabbed the steering wheel and pulled our car over to the shoulder at 65 miles per hour. The car in front of us swerved out of the way in the nick of time, and if I hadn't grabbed the steering wheel, we would have had a head-on collision.

That happened about 1970; I guess I still had a whole lot of things to do here. I've also had seven more children that wanted to come through. As I said in my book, *You'll See It When You Believe It*, things that seem to be part of our mundane affairs are really each a miracle. I've had all kinds of unusual experiences show up pretty regularly in my life, but when they happened, I haven't usually realized that they were extraordinary. It's only when I've stopped to put it all together that I've realized that there's something guiding all this, there's something happening here. We are not alone.

That's why I don't agonize over death. When you think of eternity, then death isn't a meaningful concept. We come from nowhere to now here, and back to nowhere.

WARREN FARRELL

I feel that the fact that I was created at all is a most unusual occurrence. If my parents had made love a tenth of a second earlier or later, I wouldn't exist. When I think of that, I feel the blessing of just being given life and what an enormous miracle that is.

Sometimes I have a feeling, when I look back on my life, that all I've been through has prepared me perfectly for just what I'm doing now. My original background as a feminist and political scientist, followed by my studies in psychology and sexology, all seem like crucial ingredients in helping explain why the recent imbalance between the sexes (compassion for women and anger toward men) needs to be corrected, and how it can be corrected on both a personal and a political level. My sense of being guided through this background as if by an outside force makes me feel that I'm being directed to play a particular role in the universe that I was sent out to play. When I experience this, it fills me with a sense of meaning and purpose.

WILLIS HARMAN

Some of my inner experiences have been so profound that they leave me silent and marveling—startled at a revelation of Reality that is breathtakingly new and yet realizing that "I always knew this"—and wondering how I could possibly have forgotten. As for outer experiences, these are mainly of the form of "meaningful coincidences," which are tremendously reassuring to me but not evidential to anyone else.

RICHARD HATCH

Several years ago, I injured my back badly while trying to do rolls on a high wire. I did about 400 of them one day and my back spasmed. Despite the incredible pain, I chose to get on a plane to go to Vegas to perform at the Circus of the Stars, where I was scheduled to be part of a high-wire act. While I was in Vegas, a friend of mine held me and loved me; she was there for me 24 hours a day. In that vulnerable state where all my defenses were down, I finally opened up completely to being loved.

At the Circus of the Stars, I managed to stretch enough to stand and get up on the wire. From that moment on, it was as if something lifted from me: all of a sudden I found myself able to walk on the wire. When I tried my first roll, I missed and ended up grabbing the wire by one finger, but I managed to pull myself back up on the wire, and did the roll the second time perfectly. It was as if my act was all choreographed perfectly by God. People who saw it said, "My God, did you plan it that way just to make it exciting?" I said, "I don't think that's something you can plan." It was one of my most magical experiences. The doctors had said my back was going to take at least six months to heal, but within a couple of days my back was fully recovered.

LOUISE HAY

I am just a simple woman and I have developed a simple outlook on life: *love yourself and watch the miracles begin to happen.* In my early years I suffered many traumas, yet I always came through them. What I often thought was the end of my life I see now was just another learning experience. Surviving can be a miracle in itself. Every day I ask for a deepening of my own understanding of Life. As I continue to learn and grow, my faith in a Power far greater than I am gets stronger, and I feel at more peace with this experience called life.

Jerry Jampolsky

Recently, a man thanked me for being the inspiration behind reconciliation to his brother after five years of anger and separation. They met for lunch, and the whole problem healed in a second. A week later, his brother was killed in an automobile accident. I think stories like that help people ask themselves, "Do I still want to be king of the procrastinator's club?"

I know a woman whose 19-year-old son was murdered by a person who got drunk one night. After several years, she recognized that she was living her life with the purpose of revenge. Her hair was falling out, and she was coming down with many diseases. She hated the man who killed her son, but her inner voice said she needed to make amends with the murderer. One day I went to visit her and learned she was visiting her son's murderer. When I got to his cell, I found that she was holding hands with him. There was no animosity in her anymore. She even helped get the man out of prison. People like her serve as teachers to us. They show us what's possible. They can inspire us to think, "Well, I can do that too."

Gurucharan Singh Khalsa

There's a whole realm of experience that I would call psychic. Psychic phenomena are simply higher abilities of the mind. They are often considered "spiritual," but I think of them as just distractions to the spirit. They tend to build up people's sense of power. I've had many such experiences. In fact, I used to be involved in psychic experiments with Stanley Krippner and Thelma Moss at U.C.L.A. People seek out such experiences and use them to affirm that they're making spiritual progress. Yet most spiritual writings warn against them because they can be so distracting.

For me, the greatest miracle is experiencing what is called "awakened sleep." That's when you feel the Infinite and the finite in each moment. You know what you need to know at the time you need to know it—for the higher purpose you have in mind. All the spiritual and psychic powers serve you because you're doing something that's simple, true, and righteous. It's very human. In fact, it's the essence of being human. It's very heart-centered. It's a beautiful state to be in.

EMMETT MILLER

When I was going through my agnostic period, I had a religious friend who had tried to convince me to become a fundamentalist and follow Jesus. It sounded good on paper: I thought I wanted to put all my cares in the arms of Jesus and sail off into the sunset. So I sat alone in my room one night and said to God, "Listen, I'm about to go to medical school, but I'm willing to go into the ministry and believe in you, yet I need a little help. I want a favor from you." I took out my pen and I put it on the table and I said, "I want you to turn that pen into a pumpkin just for a minute, and I promise I'll never tell anybody. You do that for me and you've got yourself a good hard worker. I'll forget medical school. But first you've got to work with me, God."

Well, God didn't come through, so I shrugged my shoulders and went to medical school. About fifteen years later, I discovered something that St. Augustine said: "To have Faith is to believe in that which you do not see, and the reward of faith is to see that in which you have believed." Well, I see that as I've changed and developed my faith, my children's lives have changed dramatically. My oldest son in particular created a whole new life for himself. From having major personal and scholastic problems, he has become an NBC news anchor in Chicago. But that's not the important thing.

As part of his new sense of himself, my son often feels drawn to buy an arm load of sandwiches and to pass them out to the homeless. Then he sits and has lunch with them. One day after he gave a sandwich to a hungry fellow, another homeless person came along and asked if he could have some. The first very hungry man broke his sandwich in half and gave it to the second man, although he did not know him. My son said he looked in this man's eyes and he reported to me, "Dad, I saw God." He underwent a transformation at that point in his life, and now he's very much on the path. To come from where we came from—the cold inner city of New York—to where he and I are now is clearly a miracle to me.

DAN MILLMAN

Some people, when they "miraculously" get healed of a disease, or win a football game, or get another desired object, they think God did it for them. Well, maybe so, but they don't much like to contemplate that when they get a terminal disease or lose a loved one, God did that for them, too. God is supposed to be only nice and good. This question "Have you experienced any miracles?" implies that God exists over and against something else, that God has certain qualities and not others (which we ascribe to the Devil.) I've had very good and very painful occurrences. I see them all as God, and while I don't look forward to having painful experiences, I thank God for all of them.

My experience of God is my experience of eating breakfast, sitting on the toilet, making love, and taking out the trash. To me, God is here and there, up and down, in and out, high and low. Other people or events can shake us out of our usual stupor enough to experience "miraculous" occurrences, but in my life, that simple opening of feeling, and remembrance is the miracle itself. I don't need to have miracles to have faith. Faith is the miracle. And I thank you for giving me the opportunity to contemplate this miracle once again.

PAM OSLIE

I can actually do magic things because of my understanding that we are co-creators with God. We can create anything we want, so I've been able to bend spoons and do psychic readings; I experience miracles constantly. It's made life more fun and God less scary to me—it feels as if we have a partnership. What amazes me is that I can experience miracles daily but later begin to doubt God. I remember this happened in the Bible after Moses parted the Red Sea. After those people had been on the other side of the sea for a while, they began to doubt God's power. That happens to me. It's strange!

As far as specifics go, little things happen all the time: when I ask for something, it may just show up in the mail, or a person will call when I'm thinking of him or her. A dramatic thing happened about a year ago when a really close friend of mine was in a severe car accident. All the doctors said he wasn't going to make it. I said to myself, "There's no chance this person is going to leave." On the way to visit him in the hospital, I prayed and visualized a guardian angel. By the time I got there, the police and the doctors said, "We don't know what happened, but it's a miracle he's alive."

When I see miracles, it makes me trust in a loving God rather than a God that says, "I don't care what you want." If I've got a desire, that's God's desire working through me. There's no separation between us, so it's okay for me to have those desires.

PETER RUSSELL

Have I experienced any miracles? God, yes! I think it's all summarized in one word: synchronicity. The more I'm in touch with the divinity inside myself, the more miraculous life becomes. If I go away on a meditation retreat, the few days following after I return are amazing: everything seems to happen as if there's a hundred angels standing behind me, orchestrating the world carefully so that everything works out absolutely perfectly. It's quite miraculous, from little things like the right phone call coming through at the right second to bumping into the right person on the street. These things shift the direction of my life for the better.

I've developed three principles that seem to go along with synchronicity. First of all, synchronicity seems to happen when I'm feeling centered. If I come off a meditation retreat, synchronicity is abundant in my life. If I'm fatigued or uptight, there's hardly any synchronicity at all. The second thing is that synchronicities seem to support my own intentions for life. If, for instance, I'm working on a book, the synchronicities that manifest are ones that lead me to find just the right material for the book. Finally, I've noticed that the more I play in the world, the more synchronicity happens. If I'm sitting in a cottage in the middle of the woods, there's very little synchronicity; it comes only through human interaction.

What I find most remarkable about synchronicity is the fact that it happens at all. The two synchronous events are completely inexplicable in any cause-effect mode of explanation; yet the fact that they happen in my life is absolutely undeniable. They act as a continual reminder that there is a higher-order principle in the universe.

BERNIE SIEGEL

As a four-year-old I almost died while choking on a toy I had taken apart and put in my mouth. I remember having the sense that dying was very peaceful. I wasn't upset that I was dying; I was only upset that my mother would be mad at me for dying. I felt very peaceful and spiritual. And just before I died, gasping for breath and being unable to call for help because the toy was caught in my larynx, I vomited, and the force threw the toy out. I was able to breathe again. My immediate thought was, "Who did that? Why was I saved? I must have something else to do in my life." I had a real sense of God, that He had decided I was not supposed to die.

As a physician, I see a lot of similarities in what we might label miracles, or what physicians call spontaneous remissions. I find the patients who undergo them have a spiritual quality, a peace of mind. That doesn't mean they haven't used what medicine has to offer, too. You know the old saying, "God helps those who help themselves." But I do know people with cancer who have gone home to die, saying, "I left my troubles to God," and their cancer simply disappeared.

Every person is a miracle. I just look around me with a view of an extraterrestrial, and I suddenly encounter miracles and beauty. I encounter that same beauty in an operating room: I cut somebody open, and the wound heals. That's a miracle. When I look at a newborn baby, I'm in awe of this miracle. I keep my baby pictures around my home and work-place. I suggest others do the same as a way of remembering the miracle that they are.

One thing on a very personal level that's affected me is finding pennies. I have always felt that God would give me a sign when I was on the right path, and for me, it's finding pennies. I know it sounds crazy, but I mean it. So if I pull into a gas station wondering if I should stop there, and I see a penny on the ground, I know I'm in the right place. Maybe God knows when we need a little boost, so He says, "I'm here. You're on the path. Here's a sign."

Brother David Steindl-Rast

When my mother was alive, she belonged to a little prayer circle. She asked the people in that circle to pray over her because she had very bad arthritis in her spine and was experiencing tremendous pain. Within days of their praying for her, the pain simply disappeared. For the rest of her life (about fifteen years) the pain never returned. Yet each time her doctor examined her he always said, "Oh, I'm so sorry, you must have great pain," as if nothing had changed at all.

When these things occur, they don't affect me in a special way; I'm not very surprised at them. I just say, "That's the way it works." Many of these unusual experiences are not really so connected with what is truly religious. What is truly religious is our relationship with our true Self. Miracles are simply phenomena that are yet unexplained. They force us to expand our noetic frame of reference.

Marsha Sinetar

Have I experienced a miracle? Yes. The holy condition. That through God's grace (and certainly through no particular merit of my own) I realize myself alive in the Living God, within the existential context of my totally ordinary life. This is utterly incredible, an extreme gift of grace and the sweetest, most charming reconciliation, next to which all other material or physical blessings pale.

Ron Smotherman

In 1984 I had an encounter with death. My life hung in the balance during a murder attempt. An extremely bright, clear light appeared and offered me the opportunity to stay in the world or come along with it (it did not specify where, but simply posed the question, "Will you come now or later?") Because of incompletions in my life, I chose to stay in the world, and in the next moment the murder weapon was broken. I experienced ecstasy, boundless love, acceptance, and infinite knowledge—all beyond description.

As a result of this encounter, I consider God to be a truly separate and powerful entity with the ability to grace anyone at any time. Since this experience, I've spoken with others who have had similar experiences. Many of these people were not even dying; one person was merely looking at his cat. In the seminars I lead, about one out of every 15 people have had such an experience. I believe that this kind of experience awaits us all at the end of our lives. Life is but a training opportunity in preparation for this eternal experience in a more substantial reality.

CHARLES TART

I'll tell you about a miracle. Once I arranged to pick up a man I had met at a conference, go to a coffee shop, and talk for an hour or two. While driving to his place in Berkeley, I suddenly got totally paranoid. I became obsessed with the belief that if I met this man at his house, I'd probably be shot. I kept thinking of people with guns beating up others. It was so intense that three times I pulled over and got ready to make a U-turn to drive home. Now, another part of me was being the clinical psychologist and saying, "Well, you passed for normal all these years and now we discover that underneath you're a total paranoid schizophrenic; a clinically very interesting case." Another part of me was just so terribly ashamed of giving into my totally irrational fear and craziness. Well, I didn't let myself make the U-turn, and I finally got to the street. The man I was going to meet was standing in front of his house, and we soon reached the coffee shop. Naturally, I did not tell him about my "psychotic" episode on the way over.

A couple of weeks later I got a letter from him in which he mentioned that, right before we went out to the coffee shop, he had become obsessed with thoughts about gangs and getting shot. Then he added, "And incidentally, did you know that they kidnapped Patty Hearst right down the block after we left?" So

I wasn't paranoid. The Symbionese Liberation Army was in the neighborhood. They beat up people with their rifle butts and they shot up the neighborhood with cyanide tipped bullets. Some part of me was tuned into Reality and trying to say, "You're going to a dangerous area." I just interpreted it as crazy.

This kind of parapsychological phenomena, both the ones I've studied in my own laboratory and spontaneous ones I've had, are real reminders to me that materialism is not the complete answer. You can't reduce the human mind to the nervous system. There are things that happen that simply can't be explained in that way. My hope is that someday we will have a more enlightened science that can help the spiritual refine itself, as well as a more enlightened spirituality that can help science move on to higher levels.

MARIANNE WILLIAMSON

My greatest miracle is that I'm happy. I have wonderful people in my life. I have the most fabulous daughter. I have the coolest career. I have so much to be thankful for. Life is very good.

At one time, the archetype for spiritual awakening was God striking Paul on the road to Damascus. I don't think that's the spiritual zeitgeist of our time. Our generation's learning curve is different. We're in a process that started accelerating in the sixties and has been accelerating ever since. Things are getting darker now, but they're also getting lighter. The public conversation is beginning to expand. We're starting to proclaim what we know to be true in our hearts. I think transformational work will be to the nineties what rock and roll was to the sixties.

"Oh Lord my God, I cried to thee and
thou didst heal me."
PS. 30.2

10
My Spiritual Advice Is . . .

"Come near to God; He is your friend."
SHINTO SAYING

The contributors enjoyed this question. After all, most of us like giving advice. Unfortunately, few of us enjoy hearing it. Especially when it comes to spirituality, people often get defensive about anything that sounds even remotely like advice. Yet this question allowed the interviewees to express what they felt other people really needed to know.

In any long-term endeavor, there will be good times and bad times. When a business begins to go sour, managers often sound the battle cry "let's get back to basics." In business, the fundamentals are such items as cash flow, customer satisfaction, and effective marketing. In the realm of the spirit, the "fundamentals" are not as clearly delineated. The purpose behind this question is to help us re-connect with the most important aspects of the spiritual path. Remember the connect the dots drawings you used to do as a child? What looked like a random assortment of dots on a page would, once all the dots were connected in the right order, turn into a very clear picture. In the same way, the many "dots" of advice offered here may seem random at first, but when taken together they paint a beautiful picture of the way we can grow spiritually.

In reading over the answers to this question, I sensed the incredible value they held for people just beginning to explore spirituality. Whenever possible, it's good to learn from people who have already traveled the roads we wish to take. The timeless truths offered here could save you or someone you love many years of trial and effort.

If you had one piece of advice to give to someone who wanted a deeper relationship with God, what would you tell them?

LYNN ANDREWS

To form a deeper relationship with God, you have to ask for something to come in. My teacher, Agnes Whistling Elk, has told me many times that you have to become receptive to your prey. That means you have to make a place within yourself for your prey to live. When I say "your prey," I mean anything that you might be looking for. If, for instance, you're looking for a guardian angel or an ally, you have to make a place within yourself that is receptive to that energy.

When I wrote *Medicine Woman*, Agnes told me that the marriage basket had been stolen from her, and she wanted me to return it to the Dreamers. So she taught me how to hunt and how to make a place within myself for the marriage basket to live. I learned how to be fully open to receiving the gift of the marriage basket, just as we must all become receptive to the gift of God's presence. Some people I talk to tell me they simply don't feel the presence of the Great Spirit in their lives. But as I talk to them longer, I realize that they have so much doubt, anger, and confusion that there's no place for God to live inside of them. They haven't become receptive to their prey. It's necessary to create a place within ourselves where God can live.

MARILYN ATTEBERRY

Love yourself; surround yourself with friends to remind you how perfect you are.

PAT BOONE

In forming a relationship with God, what we have to do is to really get ourselves "in neutral" and seek His will rather than our own. If you can get yourself out of the way and genuinely seek to find the will of God, He can shape your thinking and lead you to the right kind of decisions. We don't always know exactly what God's will is, but if we can just decide that we want it, whatever it is, it's easier to ascertain his will and come much closer to it.

Though we can learn something from the example of others, our own prayer lives should never be purely imitative, or static, or ritualistic. They should be growing and innovative and changing and fun! Come up with your own style! Invent! Create—that's one of your God-given characteristics. So spend some time in prayer, both asking for general forgiveness and cleansing and being specific about individual acts that you want to be washed away and corrected.

JOAN BORYSENKO

I would remind readers of the words of the Greek Orthodox priest, Kido Coleander, who was once asked what monks did all day long in the monastery. He replied, "We fall and get up again, fall and get up again." I think the most important thing in forming a deeper relationship with God is to be gentle and loving with ourselves and to recognize that we are made up of both light and shadow. Accepting all of who we are is probably the most difficult, and yet the most beneficial, spiritual practice.

What I would specifically tell a person would depend on the person, and where that person was in his or her life and faith. In terms of my own gradual awakening to God's Presence, I needed first to heal the wounds of childhood that left me feeling unworthy of my own love or anyone else's, never mind God's! Second, I needed an understanding that God was complete and perfect love, a forgiving God. After all, who wants a relationship with a bogeyman or a cosmic Peeping Tom? Third, I needed to know that God was both immanent and transcendent within and beyond—that the Divine truly dwells behind every pair of eyes, including my own; that I would see and know God in moments when I was truly open to giving or receiving love. Finally, once the stage was set, the most important thing for me was asking for help in knowing God. By this, I mean praying things like, "I want to know You, I want to love You, I want to be of service. I'm sick and tired of feeling scared, alone, and judgmental. Please reveal yourself to me." You see, I'm a great believer in free will. As much as the Mystery may want to enfold us in its love and wisdom, we have to want it too. Ask and you will receive— still good advice 2,000 years later.

LEVAR BURTON

My advice for forming a deeper relationship with God would be to create a quiet space within and ask the question, "How can I have a deeper relationship with you?" Then listen for an answer. The other way would be to bring playfulness and enjoyment into your spirituality. When it comes from a joyful place, it's more natural, and you'll feel more like pursuing it.

MANTAK CHIA

The first thing people need to do in forming a deeper relationship with God is open the energy channels inside themselves. The body is the temple of God. If you want to make a connection with the Tao, with God, you have to open the energy blockages within yourself. That helps make your body a conductor for God's energy. This can be done through proper meditation. The second thing you need to do is eat natural, nutritious food. A third thing you need to do to connect with God is to learn to have good thinking and good virtue. And lastly, you need to retain sexual energy. If you lose all your energy through sex, you won't have enough energy to connect with the Tao. If you consider monks, nuns, holy men, you will realize they all refrain from sex. This helps them retain more energy so they can connect with God.

DEEPAK CHOPRA

You need to find an outlet for your love, a place where you can give it freely. The more openly you experience love, on whatever terms, the closer you will come to finding its essence. Love that doesn't flow is no love at all; it is just yearning and longing. The renowned mythologist Joseph Campbell pointed the way for expressing love when he said, "Follow your bliss." Bliss is the tingling rush of love in action, the flow of Being as it reaches out to meet itself and curl back with delight in contact. Love wants to find itself, and when the circuit is complete, bliss flows. Nothing is more important than reconnecting with your bliss. Nothing is as rich. Nothing is more real.

ALAN COHEN

I would tell people who want a deeper relationship with God to follow their heart and trust that their deepest longings and intuitions are coming from Spirit. God is trying to work through us, and we just need to open a channel and let it happen. It helps to make the connection between what your intuition tells you and the results that follow.

Knowing God is like the hot-and-cold game that we used to play as children. A child would walk into a room where something was hidden, and people would say, "You're getting warm, warmer; you're getting cold, now you're freezing," and so forth. Life is always giving us feedback about whether we're following our true paths. If we're following our true, joyful voice, we are in a state of great creativity. People will receive what we have to offer, and the universe will support us for it. We need to start making associations between what we're feeling and the kind of results we're getting.

The other suggestion I have is to define God as love and only love, and to start to associate such attributes as perfection and wholeness with God. Then work to shift your identity from limitation to perfection and wholeness. See yourself as a wholly God-like being. Even if you feel sick, there's a part of you that's always whole and perfect and is never touched by illness. The more you identify with that part of you, the more you'll feel whole.

STAN DALE

There's an adage that I've lived by for many years. It says, "If God wanted to hide, God would hide in human beings because it's the last place we would think to look." So to find a deeper relationship with God, look inside, always look inside.

RAM DASS

God is always present in our lives, and it's only the veils of our own minds that keep us from appreciating that presence. One strategy you might use for obtaining a deeper relationship with God is to think of God as an imaginary playmate, and to imbue that playmate with all the qualities you would like God to have: infinitely wise, funny, loving, compassionate, etc. Then just hang out with your imaginary playmate the same way a child does. Talk with your playmate, and just be with it as if it's always there with you. Having a friend with all these wonderful qualities will make you want to move closer to it by changing your own qualities. Finally, you change enough so that you realize that your friend was real and you were imaginary—because, after all, there is only God.

When I asked my teacher, Neem Karoli Baba, "How can I get enlightened?" he said, "Serve people." When I asked, "How can I know God?" he said, "Feed people." He went on to say what Christ said: "Whatever you do to the poorest people, you're doing to me." In a way, service to another person exists on two levels. It rises out of dualism as a vehicle to come to God. It's a devotional practice of serving the Beloved, and it's known as Karma Yoga. Mother Teresa describes it by saying, "I only serve my beloved Christ in all His distressing disguises." So that's a practice, but as you merge more into the Oneness, there's no longer anybody to serve but yourself—because there's only one of us. When your foot gets hurt, your hand will naturally do what it can to relieve its pain. In the same way, as you lose your sense of separateness, the spontaneous generosity of the heart comes forth.

BRUCE DAVIS

Getting closer to God is a matter of setting priorities. We have to give our spiritual self time and space. We have to take the time to meditate and pray. For most people, their souls are their last priority; God is at the bottom of their list. This is because people don't commonly know the fruits of the spiritual life. They look for those fruits in transient, temporary pleasures. So the first step is to realize that the fruits of the spiritual life are truly satisfying.

I think for most people, spirituality is a pretty intellectual thing—but that's not really what it is. I believe that devotion is the core of the experience of spirituality. It's a very expansive love. But most people, even "spiritual" people in our culture, don't know this experience of devotion. The closest thing to this experience would be the devotion we feel toward our children, or towards our partners. If you multiply that by 100, then you have a sense of what devotion toward God is like. And devotion is what really opens up the heart. Unless the heart is totally involved, we do not really find God.

WAYNE DYER

I think of the words of Melville when he said that God's one and only voice is silence. If people want to get closer to God, they really have to learn to quiet down their inner dialogue. They say that people have 60,000 thoughts a day, every single day. And most the thoughts we have are the exact same thoughts that occurred yesterday. Rather than our being a servant of the mind, the mind needs to be made a servant to the higher part of yourself. It was Pascal who said, "All man's troubles stem from his inability to sit quietly in a room alone."

By emptying the mind through meditation, you begin to realize you're not what you think about—that there is a part of you that can *watch* what you think about. Sometimes I ask patients who are depressed, "Are you sure you know that you're depressed?" When they say, "Yes, I absolutely know," I ask them, "What about the knower? What about the part of you that observes your depression? Is he depressed as well?" You see, that's the entry point for beginning to realize that there is some part of you who can observe yourself. That "witnessing" part of yourself is the doorway to another realm.

WARREN FARRELL

I would tell those who want a deeper relationship with God to go inside themselves and tune into their feelings. Pay attention to your dreams, to what's worrying you, to the tension points inside your body and what triggers them. What your inner self is bothered and motivated by is your inner God speaking. God is all the accumulated wisdom you've gathered in your lifetime. Your body can give you something like a computer printout of this wisdom when you pay attention and listen to it.

WILLIS HARMAN

The only advice I could give is, "Let go of all preconceived notions; admit to yourself that there might be a Mystery far beyond anything you have ever imagined; trust without limit."

RICHARD HATCH

To all those looking for a deeper relationship with God, I say: Breathe. I know this may sound very simplistic, but most people breathe in a very shallow manner, suppressing not only their oxygen intake but their ability to feel, receive love, and experience their aliveness. They do this because they have been hurt, traumatized, and abused, and they don't want to feel these emotions. They are too painful. Unfortunately, this cuts them off from feeling and experiencing God in their lives. Most people try to find God by going within, moving out of their body. Although this can be quite blissful, sooner or later they have to open their eyes and deal with the world.

All my life I have been praying, meditating, going within to find peace, light, and love. I wanted to escape the world. To me, the world was a very scary and painful place. I now know that I am in the world for a purpose: to live a healthy, abundant, and joyous life. I have discovered that the key is reopening my heart, letting go of everything that has taught me not to trust, love, and value who God created me to be. When my heart is free, unburdened, open to receiving love, I experience God. When I express this love energy in the world, I become a sacred artist translating God's energy into expression.

LOUISE HAY

I suggest that those who want a deeper relationship with God release all judgment, practice forgiveness whenever they can, and learn to truly and deeply love themselves, for as their self-love deepens they will find the tremendous Power and Essence of Life that many call God. This Life Essence lies within each and every one of us.

JERRY JAMPOLSKY

The first thing I'd say to anyone who wants a deeper relationship with God is that I don't have any advice because I don't know what's best for another person. All I can do is share my own journey and what has worked for me. In my own case, I've learned to recognize that I have a particulary stubborn ego with a long history of having its own way. Most of my life I was a militant atheist. At 50 years old, I had recently gone through a bitter divorce, and I was an alcoholic as well. Reluctantly, I came across the books known as *A Course in Miracles*. While being introduced to the *Course*, I heard an inner voice say, "Physician, heal thyself. This is your way home."

I had a lot of problems with the books because of the Christian terminology it used. I had been raised in the Jewish faith. But as I did its daily lessons, I noticed I had a willingness to let go and forgive. I began to feel an inner peace that I had-n't had before in my relationships. I became aware that my purpose in life is to be a messenger of love. I also realized that to grow in this love, you have to give it away. I was guided to start a place known as *The Center For Attitudinal Healing* which embodied the principles of forgiveness, giving, and uncondi-tional love. By attempting to live these spiritual principles, my whole life began to be transformed.

GURUCHARAN SINGH KHALSA

There's hardly a formula for spiritual growth that would apply to everyone. Yet, there's two sayings I often give people, say-ings that I think are useful. The first one is "let go and let God." Effort will take you only so far. There's always a gap when you're trying to reach infinity. You can count forever and not reach infinity. The maximum experience the mind can have is the concept of God—but not the experience of God. There is always a gap. To cross that gap, you need to be able to surrender.

The second saying is "Knowing the truth is a great virtue; liv-ing it is infinitely better." The emphasis always has to be on action. You have to act Godly, and think Godly. To penetrate to your core, you need a mind that is willing to be committed to your soul. Insofar as your mind is whole and supports love, you'll perform the actions that will help you to experience the Infinite.

THE DALAI LAMA

The essence of all religions is love, compassion, and tolerance. Kindness is my true religion. No matter whether you are learned or not, whether you believe in the next life or not, whether you believe in God or Buddha or some other religion or not, in day-to-day life you must be a kind person. When you are motivated by kindness, it doesn't matter whether you are a practitioner, a lawyer, a politician, an administrator, a worker, or an engineer: whatever your profession or field, deep down you are a kind person.

Love, compassion, and tolerance are necessities, not luxuries. Without them, humanity cannot survive. If you have a particular faith or religion, that is good. But you can survive without it if you have love, compassion and tolerance. The clear proof of a person's love of God is if that person genuinely shows love to fellow human beings.

KENNY LOGGINS

The journey to the Spirit is the path inward, and we are all upon it. Some choose straighter paths than others, but we are all headed to the same place. To hear the Spirit more clearly, learn to hear the voice of intuition. To hear the intuition more clearly, learn to feel your life.

Nothing cuts us off from God, but the ego/mind can make us feel pretty badly. It can give us a false sense of isolation and unlovability. At times like these all Light is just a vague memory. Stay in the pain, in your heart, and ask for help.

EMMETT MILLER

To form a deeper relationship with God, create a silent space within, which often means creating a silent space for yourself in the world. You need to quiet the distracting noise around you so that you can hear a "voice" within that silent space. As the Chinese say, "Create a beautiful garden and the birds will come."

In order to create an inner silence, you need to discover what "efforting" and "doing" is, and give yourself permission to stop that. It's important to find a discipline, whether it be meditation, self-hypnosis, listening to music, communing with nature, tantric sex, whatever, which facilitates that quieting. You need to discover which discipline resonates most deeply with you and begin to work within the framework of that discipline. Be able to make a change when something inside says, "This is no longer the right path for you."

A student once asked a Zen master to say something very philosophical and deep about Zen. The master said, "Attention." The student was disappointed and asked for something a bit more profound. The Zen master responded, "Attention, attention." That pretty much says it all. Any discipline that guides you to be more here and now, and helps you to sand off the encrusted layers of civilization, is a good method. Ultimately, you'll begin to expose the diamond within.

DAN MILLMAN

I'd advise anyone who wants a deeper relationship with God to do the work of consciousness—to clear those internal obstructions in the body, mind, and emotions that bind attention to the self. Once the body finds relative balance (or at least, freedom from pain); once the mind lets go of its addiction to thought; once we accept our emotions and rise above fear, sorrow, anger, up into the heart, we notice what has always been with us, in us, around us, living us, breathing us, loving us, sustaining us. Ultimately, words can only point toward it.

EDGAR MITCHELL

My one piece of advice to those desiring a deeper relationship with God is that if you search for God, you will find it. It is there, right within yourself. We are already creating our reality, and that's part of the divine function. The reason it's hard for some to find God is that most of our ideas about God were imprinted at a very early age. Later information we receive about ourselves and the universe is often rejected because it doesn't match up with what we were taught as young children. We tend to interpret new information in accordance with our early ideas. So to find God, we first have to become aware of our programmed concepts of God and change them if they don't match up with our present day experience.

Many techniques have evolved for changing our outdated beliefs and concepts. Perhaps the most profound way is through hypnotherapy and the use of other altered states of consciousness. Such practices help one to find the source of behaviors and beliefs that we don't like and to modify them at the subconscious level. Other methods, such as meditation and contemplation, can also be useful in that they help one to still the mind and listen for that small voice within. To me, when you're in touch with the peace that passes all understanding, you're in touch with the divine reality.

PAM OSLIE

To you who want a deeper relationship with God, I say: Be still. In this culture, we haven't learned how to be quiet. "Be still and know that I am God." I believe when we are still, we can experience our connection and oneness with God.

PETER RUSSELL

In searching for a deeper relationship with God, I would tell people to relax. I use "relax" to refer to many different dimensions. To me, getting in touch with the experience of God is a question of letting go. It's what the Indian teachings talk about as non-attachment. They talk about letting go of our desires, letting go of our beliefs and preconceptions. When that happens, we naturally experience ourselves as we are—without the self-talk in our heads that keeps us from our experience of God. For me, relaxation is the essence of letting go—relaxation of the body, mind, heart, and soul; relaxing all the different parts of our being. Meditation is the art of relaxing all our different dimensions. Besides relaxing the body, meditation relaxes the mind from all its caught-upness in worldly thoughts; it relaxes the heart so we can experience forgiveness and compassion. When we learn to relax our attention, we begin to experience the inner world more clearly.

On a very practical level, the greatest difficulty with spiritual techniques is remembering to practice them. For that, I find community is important. If the people I interact with on a social level are following a similar path, we can remind each other of what our lives are about. Teachers can also be important, but, to a large extent, I think we can all be teachers to each other. Only five percent of us may be Masters, but there are thousands of us. We can serve as valuable reminders to each other.

BERNIE SIEGEL

One of the things that happens when you get into heaven is you're asked, "would you like to be introduced to God?" If you say "yes" then the next question is, "How would you like to be introduced?" If you say, "I've been president of such and such a company, or I raised five children," they say, "no, that's not *you*. We need to know who *you* are." The ultimate answer is, "I am a portion of God, so God already knows me—I don't really need an introduction." God and I are one, and as one minister I know said, "God is in production, and I'm in distribution, so we're all in the same system."

People simply need to be aware of what is already there. They don't need to develop a relationship with God; they just need to be aware of it. I think it's just our intellect that gets in the way of such a relationship. The Bible tells us that God speaks to us in dreams and visions. I think it helps to be in touch with God's language, which is not intellectual but symbolic. Being in touch with dreams and visions will help you understand and communicate with God. So pay attention to your dreams, your visions, your drawings, your intuitive side.

MARSHA SINETAR

Just turn toward God. That's all. Adjust your attention upward.
Steer your heart's movement towards That which is divine.
That is enough. Remember scripture's injunction: "Be still and
know that I am God." These lines suggest that if we simply do
this task—a *doing* which is our attentive, silent, worshipful
response—connection is assured.

BROTHER DAVID STEINDL-RAST

I would say to form a deeper relationship with God, cultivate
gratefulness in your life. I say gratefulness because that word
has not been heavily weighed down by religious jargon.
Gratefulness implicitly contains all the important attitudes
toward God that are explored in the different religious traditions. For instance, you cannot be grateful unless you Trust. If
you are distrustful, you can't be grateful. Grateful living
implies a certain trust in the goodness of God, and that is the
basis of Faith. If you are truly grateful, you remain so even
when you get something other than what you want. This
openness to getting other than what you want, this openness
for surprise, is called Hope.

Another aspect of gratefulness is mutuality, a sense of
belonging. When you thank people and are really grateful to
them, you enter into a mutuality there. For instance, with
people from some villages in Africa, when you first come to
their village, you bring them gifts. When they accept the gift
and mutuality has been established, there is a sense of belonging together. That "yes" to belonging together is really the
essence of love. So Faith, Hope, and Love are all contained in
the very simple gesture of gratefulness.

CHARLES TART

The piece of advice that I find extremely helpful is one attrib-
uted to a group called the "Sarmouni Brotherhood." It says,
"There is no God but Reality. To seek Him elsewhere is the
action of the Fall." To me, this means you need to seek for *truth*
first. Whenever you put your ideas about how things are
ahead of actually trying to see what's really there, you're
inevitably going to create trouble. No matter how you'd like
things to be ideally, you have to keep coming back and checking in with what actually *is*.

Actually, I'm not an authority on enlightenment; I'm an
authority on "endarkenment." I think that, rather than look for
truth, it's easier to start at the other end and look for error. That
is, try to see the error that you generate. By observing myself
directly, I find that I live in a constant ongoing sea of activity,
beliefs, attachments, aversions, hopes, and fears—and a lot of
the time I'm not paying attention to the simple sensory input I
get from the real world around me. Whatever truth ultimately
is, I know it's got to be more than just this constant sea of fantasies that I generate. So I start by trying to be alert for error. I
ask myself, "What kind of story am I telling myself instead of
looking at what's in front of my eyes? What kind of fear am I
holding onto instead of listening to what I can actually hear
with my ears? What kind of belief do I have about how things
should be instead of feeling my actual emotional feelings?"

It's not a matter of constantly thinking and analyzing, talking to yourself in your head about what you might have done
wrong. That just feeds the superego, causes no real change,
and can go on forever! The emphasis is simply on making a
deliberate effort to be more attentive to my moment-by-
moment sensory inputs and bodily feelings. By seeking reality
in this fashion, I find that errors come to light, but not just as
grist for endless rumination.

MOTHER TERESA

My message to the people of today is simple. We must love one another as God loves each one of us. To be able to love, we need a clean heart. Prayer is what gives us a clean heart. The fruit of prayer is a deepening of faith, and the fruit of faith is love. The fruit of love is service, which is compassion in action.

MARIANNE WILLIAMSON

Anytime I'm upset and feeling disconnected from God, the highest support I can receive from someone is their asking me, "Marianne, did you meditate today? Did you read something inspiring today? Are you attacking someone in your thoughts?" Most people don't really need advice. They just need support and discipline in doing what they already know works.

There has been a shift in the past few years from the path of the Seeker to the path of the Pilgrim. Being a seeker means you're looking for a path. But this is 1994, not 1974. Most of us generally know what our path is by now. This is a pilgrim-age, not just a search. There are other pilgrims all around us, some walk faster and some slower. Sometimes the road is easy, and sometimes the curves are treacherous—but we know where we're going, and we know it's possible to get there.

" He who created us without our help will not save us without our consent."
ST. AUGUSTINE

11
Paths to God

*"People are of different spiritual temperaments,
and therefore will approach
God in different ways."*
HUSTON SMITH

Each of us is on a journey toward a deeper communion with
our Creator. While the final goal may be the same for each
of us, there are as many roads to a deeper connection to God
as there are people. In the interviews I did for this book, I
came across many people with particularly fascinating stories
to tell about their spiritual journeys. The questions posed in
the previous chapters were designed to elicit specific spiritual
ideas and techniques that everyone could benefit from.
Another useful approach to spiritual learning is to step back
and see the bigger picture of the way God intersects with our

lives. From this "bigger picture," it's possible to learn new and different things about God and about ourselves.

The following seekers describe their rather unique spiritual journeys in an autobiographical context. In listening to their stories, I found further evidence that "the Lord works in mysterious ways." Perhaps you can find elements of your own journey in their reflections, and inspiration in their victories. I offer you the spiritual experiences of four special people in the path of the prisoner, the path of the healer, the path of terminal illness, and the path of the philosopher.

The Path of the Prisoner

Mark DeFriest has been in prison for the last twelve years. Seven of those years he has spent in solitary confinement, in a cell six feet wide by eight feet long. He never leaves this cell except for a handcuffed shower twice a week. Although his original crime was a minor burglary, his current 200-year sentence is due to having escaped from jail on many different occasions. After being given a prolonged sentence of solitary confinement, Mark began to pursue a spiritual path. Here are his thoughts.

Prisoners are typically stereotyped by the media and entertainment industry as the lowest sort of human animal. This makes for good stories, but in reality it is seldom true. There are indeed a substantial number of miscreants, immoral and ignorant men and women, in prison. Yet there are also many prisoners of exceptional intelligence and refined culture. In addition, prison holds many who are gifted spiritually. In fact, the prison environment can be instrumental in developing such growth.

If you will take a moment to reflect, you will find that in all spiritual disciplines, "enlightenment" typically occurs to the one who denies the world, who cuts himself or herself off from a materialistic frame of mind. Self-denial, fasting, hermitage, monasticism— these are the devices of the spiritual warrior. From Buddha under the bodi tree to Christ in the desert, separation from the world's material distractions is a persistent theme running through all spiritual traditions. The theory is simple: the mind is like a pool reflecting the moon. Thoughts, desires, and worldly distractions are like pebbles dropped into the pool causing ripples, obscuring the moon's reflection. The moon, God, enlightenment, is seen only dimly or not at all.

Only when we still the mind do we come closer to the spirit. In a prison cell, a prisoner is forcibly stripped of the world. After a time some welcome this and pursue spiritual insight. Some create distractions or go mad. A prison cell, after all, is no different from a monk's. The transition is painful, an accelerated lesson in life. At first you create daydreams to cope with the silence. There are no books, radio, or television. Just walls and you. You can feel yourself on the edge of collapsing into panic, descending into screech and whiny talk, struggling with the bars, trying to beat your way past them. It's just like withdrawal symptoms from drug addiction: it takes awhile to cleanse the spirit and still the mind. It also takes strength.

Your mind, after accepting stillness, fresh after the struggles of materialistic addiction withdrawal, now turns inward. You become consumed with the age-old questions: what is life about? Who am I? Why is this happening? Is there a God? Why do we exist? And on and on. You meditate. As time goes on, the ripples begin to fade, the peace becomes stronger, the pool is more gentle. You begin to hear the teacher inside you. You begin to feel God.

You cover many subjects in your musing: life, religion, and God first and foremost. In your temple of concrete and steel you spend as much time on these subjects as any monk. One day you realize that the cell you are in is not what confines you, it only isolates you. You understand that each of us is confined in a cell of flesh and blood, whether in prison or out, and that the concrete and steel no longer matter. You feel compassion for those in the "free world" who carry their cells with them and fail to realize it. They are trapped more thoroughly than you.

I have spent years in a cell, questing after truth—years of inner search, constantly thinking about the most personal questions. Yet all the pains, horrors, and deprivations I've suffered seem insignificant before the understanding of my own existence. The spirit can never be bound unless you allow it to be. It does not matter what happens to me materially. Indeed, no situation exists that cannot be used to effect a change for the better of my own spiritual consciousness.

Each of us has one thing in common: we must all one day die. None of us can avoid this. We live brief lives, filled with suffering, attempting to fulfill desires that are of no lasting account, with no thought of the meaning of our brief existence. It seems to me people should be more concerned with their lives and existence, as amazing as it is that we do exist. Yet most people go blindly through life without more than brief thoughts of their spiritual needs. Then, when death is upon them they call upon God. Why wait so long? He is within us! Within our Greater Selves, our whole lives long. It is only the material world and our chaotic mind that separates us from lasting inner peace.

Criminals are a hard breed, but all great saints and spiritual guides were hard men and women, willing to shed the world and pursue the chosen path indefatigably. The path calls for a rigid honesty more so than does the world, which calls only for a well crafted mask. As I write with authority, I do so also with humility. The mistakes made in my own past stand clear in my sight. In my situation, I have had to learn forgiveness the hard way and find compassion in place of resentment, love in place of hate. This is the path to freedom even in chains and behind concrete walls. True freedom transcends the world. True freedom comes only from seeking and finding God.

Mark DeFriest

The Path of the Healer

In 1980, Meredith L. Young-Sowers had a life-shifting experience with a nonphysical Divine Teacher. The experience so changed her life that she and her family moved to rural New Hampshire to further the work by founding Stillpoint Publishing and Institute for Life Healing. She sees her work in healing as one way to encourage people to bring Divine Love into everyday living and relationships with others.

As a healer and teacher, my greatest joy is in helping people find value in their own uniqueness, their own goodness. probably because I find it such a challenge to believe in my own. I've found that we need love in our life if we are to develop the courage to change. When we are unable to love and appreciate ourselves and our efforts, we run away from our mistakes and failures rather than learning from them. When we are critical of ourselves, we are also critical of others and our loneliness separates us from life's joy. When we are cut off from our own goodness, we are unable to be tender and vulnerable, to be introspective, to challenge old dysfunctional ways and beliefs wherever we find them, and to move into the joy of our relationships and our daily experiences.

This path of the heart is the path of healing. We can only teach from our own personal and direct experiences, and mine have seemed to be orchestrated by a "greater knowing" in response to the critical times in which we live. No matter the type of spiritual initiation we have had or in which culture it is framed, the experience shifts our perception to our inner eyes through which we become sensitive to awakening the sacred.

My initiation came about in a most unusual and unexpected way. In 1980 following months of strange inner vibrations, I was guided out of my body by an unseen Divine Master and allowed to experience the slip-stream of consciousness that connects the physical and spiritual worlds. The veil between the seen and unseen worlds of reality was lifted for a few moments and I felt Divine Grace and Love fill every pore of my loneliness and separateness with glorious joy and well-being. I have never found any Earthly experience that came even marginally close to producing these feelings.

A deep explosion of love swallowed up my pain and I saw with inner eyes the vastness and all-encompassing nature of Love as a living energy. In that flash of understanding, I realized that Love was the basis for all life and that we are all made from this single essential essence. My inner vision was clearly focused so I could easily see into dense physical matter. Even mountains and lakes, animals and trees, were created from Divine Love. While in this altered state of consciousness I knew that there were no limitations, no pain, no loss that could ever be felt in this inner place of Love. All could be healed.

I now know that this was the experience of awakening Divine Love in my heart and fully engaging my yearning to be of service to others.

One might think that by opening this doorway to Divine Love the rest of my life would have flowed with equal harmony. But the exact opposite was to be true for many years. This vision was so powerful and the on-going instruction from this Master Teacher so explicit yet so difficult to live, that for years I found no stable footing in either the world of spirit or the one of my physical experiences. In retrospect I realize I was being taught to measure life against all that I could perceive with my inner eyes rather than only through the lenses of my physical eyes and physical reality.

Many grueling years followed in which I struggled to find a synthesis of the two worlds of what I could see and touch and what I felt and perceived to be eternal. My twenty-two-year marriage dissolved, my children left home for several years, and the business that was the very essence of my life work came within a heart-beat of collapsing. Yet, I continued to learn about Universal Love as energy and the ways to use my inner sight to identify disease, dysfunction, and core life issues and themes that lead to imbalance and pain in people's bodies, emotions, and relationships with others.

I learned that we each have a largely untapped capacity to channel Divine Love to those who need healing. It took years of practice to find a familiarity with the images I saw and what they mean in actual physical terms. When I see dark or black colors in a person's physical or etheric body, I know those parts hold physical disease or dysfunction. Gray means disease is looming within the person's life and has the potential to manifest within the near future. By observing the currents of energy cascading down, over, and through a person's chakras or energy centers, I interpret the strength, color, and texture of this energy and its movement to accurately decipher a person's unresolved life issues. After years of work, I have learned to perceive the spiritual dis-ease and imbalances that are the root causes of many kinds of physical and emotional disturbances.

From the beginning, I wanted a true and enduring belief in the spiritual dimension, yet at every turn my own disbelief, ego, and fears seemed to be my downfall. Even though I was learning new skills of awareness and perception from my angelic teacher, I often felt like a failure because my own life wasn't working. I used my skill in every way possible to help others, but I resisted applying the spiritual insights to my own life. My abilities remained tools of my healing work rather than the integrated basis of my own spiritual journey.

Living in Divine Love is my daily challenge. I still find it difficult to accept that my work isn't necessarily to take away somone's pain or anguish, but to guide them through their own self-discovery. When we open our heart to love we expand our capacity to feel compassion and joy. It is from this place of honest emptiness that we surrender to a greater force within which we live. As we open our heart to Love, we find joy and pleasure in living within this universal spiritual flow.

With our physical eyes we can only see part of the universal spectrum of energy that creates physical matter. When we are centered in our heart, in the place of our spirit, we have different eyes and these can perceive the movement of energy within a physical body, within other living creatures, trees and plants, within the Earth, and within groups of people or organizations.

Everything is made of energy and when we focus our inner

eyes in ways to perceive energy, we can see the results that our positive and negative words have on other living things. We can see the basis of disease that is the accumulated feelings of loss, separation, self-criticism, and lack of love, that becomes layered in our tissues and muscles.

The journey of the heart is a lasting path to God. We find our teachers on this spiritual path as we are ready to know a little more, to try the next step, to break through an old inner limitation. The metaphor of kneading and baking a loaf of bread speaks to the subtle process we all undertake in manifesting our spiritual service into our physical life. Long before the bread is ready for us to enjoy, we have placed the right ingredients together and then kneaded the bread to increase its elasticity and to prepare it for baking. Just like the kneading process for bread, our life is a pot pourri of diverse experiences and beliefs that we seek to synthesize. We smell the incredibly delicious scent of the bread baking in the oven, but it's not yet ready to eat.

Similarly in my life as the bursts of new insight, energy, and creativity begin to emerge, I want to act on these immediately but they may not yet be fully developed enough to show the tangible picture of my spiritual action plan. As I follow my joy, trust in a greater Universe, and use Divine Love at every opportunity, the outward manifestation of my work in the world, the bread, takes a discernable form.

The spiritual journey isn't quick, or easy, but I am propelled by knowing the God within me, the Divine Love that is our essential nature. And so I walk the path that I've chosen at some deep and unknowable level. As I am able and willing to heal my own life through living in Divine Love, I become an able instrument for a greater good wanting to emerge on this Earth and in all people.

Meredith L. Young-Sowers

The Path of Terminal Illness

Jim Nissley found out he was HIV positive (the AIDS virus) in November of 1990. Since then, he has become a well-known AIDS activist. After realizing he got AIDS by using a lambskin instead of a latex condom, he led a successful drive to have warning labels put on all lambskin condoms. In December of 1992, he met with President-elect Clinton to talk about what · can be done to positively impact the AIDS situation. Jim lives in a house for people with AIDS, and is now considered a long-term AIDS survivor.

In 1980, there was a period of about four days where I lived in the possibility that I might have prostate cancer. It ends up I didn't, but the experience got me moving. Prior to that time, my life had been about acquiring physical things. After that experience, I set out to travel the world and look for God. I had gone to India a few times, and had been deeply touched by the spiritual master Sai Baba. In March of 1990, I had an extensive interview with Sai Baba in which he told me that the coming year would be the hardest in my life. He said my faith would be tested until it was unshakeable. My reply to him was, "Then I better have proof." The last thing Sai Baba said to me that day was, "I will always be with you."

On the plane trip home, I got violently sick. I was in the restroom with severe stomach cramping. I called out to Sai Baba and I heard an inner voice telling me to "use the package of virbhuti." Virbhuti is simply ashes that have been made holy by the Guru's blessing. I dumped the full contents of a small package in my hand and rubbed it on my stomach. Suddenly, I felt something. I opened my eyes and clearly saw Sai Baba in front of me. His image slowly faded, and within a couple of minutes I was totally well. But I'm a born skeptic. I thought, "I was in a lot of pain, maybe I was hallucinating." When I went to throw out the empty package of ash, I noticed that it was totally filled again. At that moment, I heard an inner voice say, "You asked for proof, you have it. Now trust." My faith was soon put to the test...

A few months later, a fire completely devoured my house and everything I owned. I had been hearing a voice in my head telling me to check on my home owner's insurance, but I had never gotten around to it. It ends up my insurance had expired. I lost everything in the fire. I remember sitting in the ruins of my house and asking myself what my life would be about now. Three months later, I was diagnosed as HIV positive. When I was diagnosed, it was the first time in my life that absolutely everything made sense. My whole life had been a preparation for what I was about to go through. I believe that the events leading up to my getting AIDS and the events that have happened since then have all occurred through divine intervention.

Soon after learning I had AIDS, I looked at a package of lambskin condoms to see if there was some kind of warning about how it didn't prevent HIV transmission. To my total shock, there was nothing. Then I went home and, as I was watching TV, an AIDS commercial came on. Basically, the commercial said you should use a condom. I figured it was a government commercial—what could you expect? But at the commercial's end, it said paid for by the San Francisco AIDS Foundation. In that moment, my whole life as I had known it halted. I realized that if I didn't take up the cause of warning people about lambskin condoms, nobody else was going to do it.

I immediately came up with a long list of reasons for not doing anything about the condom situation. First of all, I was just one person. I was sick with AIDS, I had huge medical bills, and I had just lost everything I owned in a fire. But I knew that if I didn't do something, I wouldn't be able to live with myself. I became a man with a mission. I spoke to politicians, eventually culminating in meeting with President Clinton. NBC Nightly News ended up doing a five minute story on me. Soon thereafter, the FDA seized over a million lambskin condoms for failure to warn consumers.

I nearly died in the spring of 1991. On Easter Sunday, my

doctor said that if I didn't go into the hospital, I'd be dead within 72 hours. My commitment was that I would never go into a hospital, so I simply went home and surrendered to God. I accepted the fact that I was going to die. I kept praying, not for healing, but for the ability to fully surrender to God. By the next day when I saw the doctor, I felt a lot better. After a chest x-ray and blood oxygen count, my doctor asked, "What the hell have you been doing?" It seems that my blood oxygen count had gone from 58 (risking brain damage) to 85 (fully normal) in one day. Out of being totally willing to die, God gave me the strength to choose life.

People sometimes ask me what it's like thinking you're going to die soon. My first reaction to hearing I had HIV was total panic. I thought I had accepted that I would die someday, and I thought I was at peace with that. The panic showed me that I never really got that I was going to die. We all think, "Yeah, someday way off in the future I'm going to die." Suddenly, I felt totally out of control. It's very difficult to live with the knowledge of your own mortality for more than just a short period of time. Only if you have a profound relationship with God can you be okay with your own death. Otherwise, it's just too frightening.

Our society has now made death the enemy. Society says we should want to survive no matter what. I think that just comes from our fear of death, which comes from not feeling connected to God. From living in this house (where all the residents have AIDS), I've come to realize that death is not such a bad thing. I've been with many people at the moment of their death, and during their last breath, there is always a smile. For the people who die, it seems to be a very wonderful, freeing experience. I find it interesting that the more willing I've been to die, the freer and healthier I've been to live my life.

Sometimes people have asked me, "Why don't you ask Sai Baba to cure you?" I tell them I have no desire to be cured. In fact, once Baba asked me what I wanted. I told him I wanted to "overcome my fear of death, and learn the lessons of this disease." At that point, out of thin air he materialized this ring I'm now wearing. Then he went on to say that the lessons this disease is trying to teach humanity is the importance of self-discipline and personal responsibility. Self-discipline and personal responsibility are what it would take to stop the spread of this disease. But most people would rather live in denial.

People need to be able to welcome adversity. If one is willing to take responsibility and not blame, incredible growth comes out of adversity. Blame does no good. All it does is keep us trapped. We all have our lessons. We can learn them the easy way or the hard way. To the degree that I'm willing to take responsibility for the situations in my life, the easier the lessons are to learn. I believe that the ultimate lesson is for us to be completely responsible for everything that happens in our life. Taking responsibility is our ultimate test. It's the test that frees us from the cycle of death and rebirth, and finally returns us to God.

In order to know God better, I think it's important to get present to the depths of your own despair. Trying to find lasting peace in the material world is ultimately hopeless. Our bodies get sick and die, and there's absolutely nothing that we can do about it. I am convinced that until you have a deep connection with God, there is no true joy. For me, once I stopped denying my despair and became open to another possibility, God stepped in. You don't have to go anywhere to find God. God is right here, right now. All you have to do to talk to God is speak. All you have to do to hear God is listen.

I do talks to various groups now about AIDS, taking responsibility, God, etc. People sometimes come up to me to tell me how inspired they were by the talk. I ask them, "Well, what are you doing in *your* life?" Being inspired for a moment is meaningless. We need to take consistent meaningful action. A tragedy even bigger than AIDS is the fact that most people in this country reach their death without ever having truly lived....

Jim Nissley

The Path of the Philosopher

When asked, "What do you do?" Robert Fulghum usually replies that he is a philosopher, and then explains that what he likes to do is think about ordinary things and then express what he thinks by writing or speaking or painting, whichever seems appropriate. .

"Do you believe in God, Mr. Fulghum?" (The journalist interviewing me has shifted scale suddenly from the details of dailiness to the definition of the Divine.)

"No, but I do believe in Howard."

"Howard? You believe in Howard?"

"It all has to do with my mother's maiden name."

"Your mother's maiden name . . ."

"Was Howard. She came from a big Memphis clan that was pretty close and was referred to as the Howard Family. As a small child, I thought of myself as a member of the Howard Family because it was often an item of conversation as in 'The Howard Family is getting together,' and 'The Howard Family thinks people should write letters to their grandmother.' The matriarch, my grandmother, was referred to as Mother Howard."

"And you thought . . . she . . . was . . . God?"

"No, no, I just wanted you to first know how it was that Howard was a name that was important to me from early on in my life. What happened was that I got packed off to Sunday School at around age four and the first thing I learned was the Lord's Prayer, which begins 'Our Father, which art in heaven, Hallowed be Thy name.' And what I heard was, 'Our Father, which art in heaven, HOWARD be Thy name.' And since little kids tend to mutter prayers anyhow, nobody realized what I was saying, so I went right on believing that God's name was Howard. And believing I was a member of His family—the Howards. Since I was told that my grandfather had died and gone to heaven, God and my grandfather got all

mixed up in my mind as one and the same. Which meant that
I had a pretty comfy notion about God. When I knelt beside
my bed each night and prayed, 'Our Father, which art in heav-
en, Howard be Thy name,' I thought about my grandfather
and what a big shot he was because, of course, the prayer ends
with 'For Thine is the kingdom, the power, and the glory forever and ever. Amen.' I went to bed feeling pretty well connected to the universe for a long, long time. It was a Howard
Family Enterprise."

"You're not putting me on, are you?"

"Not at all. All human images of the ultimate ground of
being are metaphors, and as metaphors go, this is a pretty homey
one. And I thought it for so long that even when I passed
through all those growing-up stages of skepticism, disbelief, revi-
sion, and confusion—somewhere in my mind I still believed in
Howard. Because at the heart of that childhood image there is
no alienation. I *belonged* to the whole big scheme of things. I
lived and worked and had my being in the family store. . ."

There was a long silence between us. The journalist smiled.
I smiled. She changed the subject. None of this discussion
about Howard appeared in her article. I understand. Some
things are hard to write about . . . hard to think about . . . hard
to sort out. Maybe when she asked the first question, I should
have just said, "Yes." As a favor to her. But the truth is I haven't
finished thinking about God, and the God of my childhood and
the God of my middle age are mixed in with the God of the wisdom that may yet come to me in my later years. Howard would
understand.

On a long flight from Melbourne to Athens, an Australian carpenter, an Indian college professor in hydrology, and I had a
memorable late-night theological discussion. The three of us
were seated in one row, and the subject of God came up because
our meals were accompanied by a little card on which was printed a short prayer of thanksgiving.

The professor made some remarks about *not* being thankful to *any* of the gods for this particular food. The carpenter composed a prayer of complaint. And the discussion was off and running.

The carpenter declared his theology had a lot to do with fleas and a dog.

Arguing whether or not a God exists is like fleas arguing whether or not the dog exists. Arguing over the correct name of God is like fleas arguing over the name of the dog. And arguing over whose notion of God is correct is like fleas arguing over who owns the dog. . . .

Later on, the Indian professor and I stood in the forward alcove of the 747 where the galley and rest rooms are, comparing the route map with what we could see out the porthole in the door.

He noted that we had just left a country where people worshipped the sun—on the beach with most or all of their clothes removed. And we were flying over countries whose people believed it was the will of Allah that women should be completely covered, even on beaches. The name of God varied from country to country; the holy book was not the same; the rituals and dogmas and routes to heaven were not the same. And so certain were the followers of the different religions of their rectitude, they would gladly war with one another—kill one another—to have their beliefs and metaphors prevail. Yet in this same plane, flying peacefully along, are these same people.

Clearly this troubled the professor—grieved him. He shook his head and asked why this must be so. Why? Why?

The professor pointed out the Indian Ocean beneath us at the moment.

He spoke of water, his specialty.

"Water is everywhere and in all living things—we cannot be separated from water. No water, no life. Period. Water comes in many forms—liquid, vapor, ice, snow, fog, rain, hail. But no matter the form, it's still water.

"Human beings give this stuff many names in many languages, in all its forms. It's crazy to argue over what its true name is. Call it what you will, there is no difference to the water. It is what it is.

"Human beings drink water from many vessels—cups, glasses, jugs, skins, their own hands, whatever. To argue about which container is proper for the water is crazy. The container doesn't change the water.

"Some like it hot, some like it cold, some like it iced, some fizzy, some with stuff mixed in with it—alcohol, coffee, whatever. No matter. It does not change the nature of the water.

"Never mind the name or the cup or the mix. These are not important.

"What we have in common is thirst. Thirst!

"Thirst for the water of Life!"

As it is with water, so is it with God.

"I don't know much about God," said the professor of hydrology. "All I know is water. And that we are momentary waves in some great everlasting ocean, and the waves and the water are one."

He poured us each a paper cup full of water and we drank.

Robert Fulghum

*"We are beings in a school for gods in which we
learn in slow motion the consequences of thought."*
WM. BRUGH JOY

Epilogue

While I was compiling this book, almost everyone I talked to asked me the same basic question: "What's the essence of the answers you're receiving?" Implied in such a question is that there is an obvious essence to be gleaned from the material. But the sheer variety of answers, methods, and points of view offered here make a "summary statement" now seem ludicrous to me. Indeed, the one thing that stood out for me in the answers was the highly individual nature of each person's responses. In many cases, I couldn't even tell what religion or spiritual beliefs the respondents held from the answers they gave. The religious labels we're used to, such as "Buddhist" or "New Ager," seemed almost irrelevant. What *did* become apparent was the notion that, through trial and error, these seekers discovered specific practices that deepen their connection to the Divine. The adage "know thyself" seems to have practical spiritual value. In pursuing their own interests and intuitions, the seekers in this book often stumbled upon ways to become more intimately merged with God.

In this fast-paced world in which we live, we're all looking for short cuts. For better or worse, deepening our connection to the Divine does not fit comfortably into our consumer-oriented society. God can't be purchased. We have to walk the long road ourselves, step by step. The people who contributed to this book have offered us their "maps" towards the "kingdom of heaven within." Yet ultimately, we all need to listen to our own hearts for the call of Divine guidance.

The Future of God

Throughout much of recorded history, "spiritual matters" were "handled" by a chosen class of people, such as priests or Brahmans, but by the Renaissance, people began to take responsibility for their own connection to God. Now that there is even more religious freedom and more spiritual methods available to us, our ability to determine our spiritual destiny is greater than ever. A sign I once saw on a church bulletin board summed up our condition aptly: "If you don't feel close to God, guess who moved?"

While conventional technology has accelerated exponentially in recent decades, the "inner technology" of evolving our own consciousness has lapsed far behind. Rather than building on each other's spiritual insights, we've bickered about the best or the right way to connect with God. Yet, as can be seen in the responses to Chapter Seven to the question, "What does God want from us?", seekers from widely different backgrounds agree basically as to what God calls us to do. This is encouraging. Once we agree collectively as to the goal of spirituality, we can learn from each others' experience as to the most effective way to get there. The "technology" of knowing God, of knowing our Divine essence, will be fully born.

As we approach the end of the second millennium, I believe that God will become a topic of considerable discussion and interest to us. In modern times, we've focused on mastering the material world as a means to a better existence;

yet even with all our amazing technology, there seems to be as much suffering today as there ever was. As our second millennium closes, perhaps we will learn to integrate our proficiency in the material world with true spiritual wisdom and vision.

A Fable

Long ago there was a mighty King who lived a sheltered and indulgent life inside the walls of his castle. One day he decided to venture into his kingdom to see what he might experience and learn. He soon came upon a monk and, in a voice accustomed to instant obedience, said, "Monk, teach me about heaven and hell!" The monk looked up at the mighty king and in an annoyed voice said, "I can't teach you about heaven and hell. You're too stupid. You're just an indulgent slob. The teachings I have are for pure and holy people. You don't even come close. Get out of my way!"

The king became furious. He was appalled that this monk dared to speak to him in this manner. In a fit of rage he pulled out his sword to chop off the monk's head.

"That's hell." said the monk confidently.

The king was stunned. He realized this courageous monk had risked his life to teach him this lesson about hell. In deep gratitude and humility, the king put down his sword and bowed reverently to the monk.

". . . and that's heaven," said the monk softly.

I wish you ever-deepening love and aliveness
in your journey toward the heart of the
Divine.

Your Personal Reflections

My hope is that the responses in this book have inspired you, as well as given you new ideas about how to experience Living Spirit. While methods are definitely helpful, more than just good techniques are needed to experience God. Besides grace, a deep desire and a sense of urgency are very helpful. I encourage you to go back and reflect on and use the suggestions that most affected you. I have found that when I meditate and pray, reading from this book helps me connect with a sense of the sacred. Sometimes I read a particular passage over and over again, until it finally becomes part of me.

What follows are a list of open ended statements to help focus your thoughts in ways that could be helpful. Just as in a relationship with a human being, our relationship to Spirit can fall into ruts and routines. I believe that if you write your answers to the following six statements, your relationship with God will become even more intimate and fulfilling.

In the past, I have experienced a divine connection when I have . . .

Of the many methods for experiencing God described in this book, the three that seemed to be the most beneficial to try are . . .

❀ ❀

Two specific practices I can do to attune more deeply into
the sacred in my daily life are . . .

❅ ❅

I feel I'm in a spiritual rut—doing things without my heart
really being in them—when I . . .

_____

_____

_____

_____

_____

_____

_____

_____

_____

_____

_____

_____

_____

_____

_____

_____

_____

_____

The one belief I could choose to have about the Divine that would help me have a more intimate connection with my Higher Power is . . .

About the Editor

Jonathan Robinson is a psychotherapist, workshop leader and professional speaker living in Santa Barbara, California. He has spent more than twenty years studying the most practical and powerful methods available for psychological and spiritual growth. He is the author of various audio and video tapes, including the number-one bestselling video, "Intimacy and Sexual Ecstasy."

If you would like a free catalog of Jonathan's audio and video tapes, or would like more information about Jonathan's workshops and public talks, please write:

Jonathan Robinson
P.O. Box 1501
Santa Barbara, CA. 93102
Fax (805) 563-4646

To Our Readers

As publishers we seek to live in ways that lighten our human load on the Earth's natural systems and our global environment.

This book is printed on chlorine-free recycled paper (minimum 10% post consumer waste) to save trees and to encourage pulp and paper companies to convert to production processes that do not create highly toxic wastes such as dioxin and other organochlorines.

The Environmental Protection Agency and many other public health agencies have found that dioxin (a by-product created when wood pulp is chlorine bleached) poses a cancer risk to humans and can have harmful effects on immune and reproductive systems of individuals.

You can help protect our air, water, and soil by requesting that the books you purchase be printed on chlorine-free recycled paper. In doing so, we both put our ecological values into actions that contribute to building a sustainable future–for our children, for generations to come, and for a healthy Earth home.

Errol G. Sowers
Publisher